T0128277

SURVIVING
Singleness
The Stress-Free Way

DR. SHIRLEY P. AUGUSTE

WESTBOW
PRESS®
A DIVISION OF THOMAS NELSON
& ZONDERVAN

WestBow Press books may be ordered through booksellers or by contacting:

WestBow Press
A Division of Thomas Nelson & Zondervan
1663 Liberty Drive
Bloomington, IN 47403
www.westbowpress.com
1 (866) 928-1240

Photographer: Charles S. Brabble, Jr. www.vividintensity.com
Makeup artist: LaVerne Bryant at L & M Hair Studio 757-374-4509

Scripture quotations taken from The Holy Bible, New International Version® NIV® Copyright © 1973 1978 1984 2011 by Biblica, Inc. TM. Used by permission. All rights reserved worldwide.

Scripture taken from the Amplified Bible, Copyright © 1954, 1958, 1962, 1964, 1965, 1987 by The Lockman Foundation. Used with permission.

ISBN: 978-1-6642-0588-8 (sc)
ISBN: 978-1-6642-0589-5 (hc)
ISBN: 978-1-6642-0587-1 (e)

Library of Congress Control Number: 2020917936

Print information available on the last page.

WestBow Press rev. date: 09/30/2020

CONTENTS

Dedication vii

Chapter 1   Why? 1
Chapter 2   Why Am I Still Single? 5
Chapter 3   There Are No Good Men or Women 7
Chapter 4   Let's Just Have Sex 13
Chapter 5   Am I the Only One Struggling? 19
Chapter 6   Challenges We Face 23
Chapter 7   Real Talk about Singleness 27
Chapter 8   What People Won't Talk About 33
Chapter 9   It's Better to Wait Than Jump In and Become
            Worse Off 39
Chapter 10 Things to Do to Avoid Pitfalls 43
Chapter 11 Waiting and Preparing 51
Chapter 12 Keys to Finding Peace and Happiness in Singleness 57
Chapter 13 Building a Strong Foundation 63
Chapter 14 Wait! I Have Children! 71
Chapter 15 Married People and Preparing to Marry 77
Chapter 16 Love 89
Chapter 17 Let It Begin 93

The Commitment Challenge 97
Daily Affirmation 99

DEDICATION

Thank you for supporting my work and reading my book. I pray you will be blessed by its contents and able to experience freedom with unsurpassed peace.

This book is dedicated to my wonderful children, Jasmin and Aaron; my parents; my brother, sisters, and their families; my extended family; my best and closest friends; my former churches for encouraging me to try to walk according to the Word; and to all the wonderful single people finding their way.

I thank my children for being my inspiration to do and be better. I never wanted them to grow up seeing a revolving door of men, so I sacrificed my desires for them. It was always heartbreaking to me when I heard stories about children resenting their parents for the number of men or women they brought home. It was even worse when I met grown folks still struggling with issues because of what they had seen growing up. As a result, I vowed to keep my kids first no matter how hard it was for me.

Thank you to the men I have learned from for teaching me the importance of not being a friend with benefits or a notch on someone's belt.

To all the single people, keep your heads up and know that you were wonderfully created! You deserve to be treated like royalty, so don't let the world make you feel that you must settle. You are not alone. I hope reading about my walk will help you stay the course to happiness and peace.

Lastly, thank you to all of the couples who have shared their story to help others understand the beauty and trials of marriage. Your words of wisdom will bless many. I am honored that you were willing to share your story. May God continue to bless your marriages.

CHAPTER 1

Why?

Singles, have you been struggling with your singleness? Are you frustrated with how people and the media view and depict single people? Why do they make it seem like something is wrong with you for being single? The entertainment world and social media portray a negative image of how singles are supposed to carry themselves. Let me see ... Single people are supposed to be promiscuous party animals, desperate people with personal issues and high expectations, or the type willing to steal others' mates. Some singles do get involved with or are tempted by others who are in relationships for many reasons, but I believe it is wrong to get involved with someone who is already involved.

The perceptions and expectations of singles are insane! No wonder some singles rush into relationships and those relationships end up being unhealthy or short-lived. Perhaps the saddest are the singles who bounce from one person to the next to fulfill their selfish needs while hurting other singles (no judgment—this is just reality).

Unfortunately, more singles than many realize are struggling with emotional hurt. I hope this book will bring some healing and guidance to all singles who want to heal their hurt and eventually enter healthy relationships. Everyone deserves to be happy.

I am not an expert on relationships, but I share my experiences here to help others find healing and peace. As a single person for over nineteen years (as of 2020), I decided to write this book to help single people know that they are not alone and that they can attain peace and experience joy. In this book, I will define what it means to be single and provide strategies for singles to find happiness and peace, avoid pitfalls, and create standards for their future mates. I will have some real talks with them, and encourage them to stand their ground and ignore others' and society's expectations of singlehood.

I'm *not* an expert; I'm a single person who has found peace and joy in my singleness. I am happily single and have reached a level of peace where I am fine with whatever the future holds for me. I do want to remarry; I want to be in love with and marry the right person for the right reasons, not just be in a relationship. I do not want to lose my peace because of constant frustration with infidelity, rudeness, or disrespect. I want to be with someone who cares enough about me to not disrespect me or allow anyone else to do so.

I want someone who is willing to work on our relationship as much as I am and do his best to work through the good and bad times. Our love for and relationship with God will keep us grounded. I want someone who will not give up on us just because things get challenging. Relationships are not easy; they require work, dedication, and a commitment to sticking around and making them work. Challenges are not excuses to cheat or throw in the towel; they are opportunities to grow and strengthen each other. Unfortunately, society tells us we should give up, fall out of love, and move on to the next person, but what society tells us to do is not always right.

Yes, you are struggling with your singleness and want to be in a healthy relationship. You wonder if something is wrong with you, and no, there's nothing wrong with you. It's human nature to want to be with someone. However, do not allow that desire to overtake you and lead you to make a decision that could cause drama or issues in your life. There are times when you will struggle with your singleness, during those times, it is important to evaluate what you are feeling. As hard as it may be, put your phone down and do not call or text anyone. Unless, it is a person that reciprocates your feelings. Your feelings are real and normal. Take the time to determine if that feeling is simply because of your fleshly desire to be in a relationship or a sign that you're not comfortable with your singleness.

Achieving peace, knowing who you are, and why you want to be in a relationship is very important before you get into a relationship. Do not be afraid of being by yourself and discovering what you like, do not like, and determining everything you want in a relationship; your long-term happiness is more important than a temporary relationship. Know who you are and what you can bring to a relationship, so you won't lose yourself in it.

Learning is not always about theory, philosophy, or talking to experts. Learning can often come from listening to lived experiences. A story of how someone overcame struggles can have a greater impact on someone than theory or philosophy can. Though any form of education or training is important and can be an effective way to learn, everything has a place. This book is going to be about real talk and real-life experiences.

Not everyone is going to agree with what I write, but that's okay; everyone's experiences are different because of culture, upbringing, faith, and choices, including reading this book. If you can relate, great! If you cannot, great! I wrote this book to help singles find peace, joy, and hope in their state of singleness. I am grateful for the opportunity to share my thoughts with those who find help and encouragement in this book, and I hope they find greater joy and peace.

Being single can be a wonderful season of your life, depending on the choices you make. I hope your choices will bring you peace and won't hurt anyone. Are you ready to learn about yourself and find peace and joy? Then let's get started. And keep an open mind as you think about life and how to become a better version of yourself.

Prayer

Father above, guide my steps and help me determine how I must grow at this stage of my life. Give me peace and guidance. In Jesus Christ's name I pray, amen.

CHAPTER 2

Why Am I Still Single?

Why are you single? I don't know. There are many reasons a person can be single. Is it a bad thing? Absolutely not. Being single is not a crime, death sentence, or curse; it's simply a stage of life. Some people are single by choice, circumstances, or for many other reasons. Some decide to stay single permanently, and that's okay if they're not defiling themselves or others sexually, manipulating, or leading others on.

To truly be single, you must not be in any sort of committed relationship, not be sexually active with anyone, not lead others on, and not have a friend or two for when you want someone just for a night. It is difficult to understand how people can say they are single if they are sexually involved with someone. Being sexually involved with another is a form of a relationship. When you involve someone else's emotions and body in some way, you're not acting in a single state of mind.

Being single is a journey of enjoying yourself and those you love (family or close friends—usually the same sex). Many might not agree with my definition of singleness; some will say that the definition is subjective, but I hope to shed light on a healthy way to be single; to help singles understand the long-term damage that can occur when they think only of themselves and their desires. It is important to understand that your actions can hurt or bless others.

Some people have not chosen to be single; that decision was made for them. Life can be unexpected and strange. One day, everything is going great, and the next, your whole world is falling apart. Similarly, you may be in a relationship or think that everything is going great, then one day, you find yourself alone. Your mate could have left in many different ways (death, divorce, infidelity, separation, abandonment, etc.).

Being unwillingly single is unfortunate and never easy; those in that state will need time to heal and adapt to this new state; that isn't easy, but it's possible. It's easy for others to tell you, "Get over it!" or "Just move on!" but the beginning of this new season of singleness might feel like a curse or even death for some, who will wonder how they are going to make it through.

If you feel that way, just know that being single is not a curse and that you will eventually get past your feelings of emptiness and loneliness in time. Everything takes time to heal. When it feels like the end of the world, ask God for strength. You don't need to make a long, drawn-out prayer; just scream or yell, "Help me!" You'll make it. You'll overcome. One day, you'll look back at this season of your life and know you made it to the other side, and you'll be amazed. Give yourself time, and do not rush the process. Don't worry about how long it will take; everyone's time frame is different. For now, you just have to take the first step and begin your healing process.

Prayer

God, open my eyes and heart to know why I am single and what you want for me to do in this state. If I have hurt or wounded anyone, please show me who and how to pray to undo the damage I've caused. Free me from any and all curses or negative karma for my foolish and immature actions. In Jesus Christ's name I claim the victory, amen.

CHAPTER 3

There Are No Good Men or Women

Many singles end up alone and believing no good men or women are out there, but I disagree. At one point in my life, I did think that men were horrible, selfish, and only out for themselves. I had a very unhealthy mind-set because of the bitterness and pain I felt. It took a lot of self-healing, discovery, and faith in God for me to realize that some of my beliefs were wrong. Once I started healing my emotions and relationships, I began to see men and women differently and understand that good men and women are out there. I've met them, honest and faithful men and women looking for someone to love them faithfully and respectfully. Are you one of those men or women?

You're probably wondering, *If good men and women are out there, then why are you, Shirley, still single?* It's because I made my share of mistakes by walking away from relationships that I should have given a chance. I was not emotionally available, and I couldn't commit to or give the relationship a true opportunity to succeed. Now, I'm at a different stage in life and am learning daily about myself and relationships. I hope to help others not make the mistakes I made. If I can help even just a handful of men and women find true love and peace and avoid hurting others, I'll have accomplished my goal. I want to see people truly in love and willing to work at their relationships. I hope those who don't desire relationships can enjoy their lives to the fullest while being celibate in their full calling for Christ.

Many singles make the mistake of getting into a relationship just because someone tells them, "This person is perfect for you!" Just because a man appears to be a great guy or a woman seems to be the perfect woman does not mean he or she is the one for you; you'll learn that only after you really get to know him or her. If you're seeing someone and things are going well in that respect, a new person is not a great option; he or she is simply a temptation to keep you from truly finding happiness and peace.

How do you know what kind of person is great for you? You first have to know who you are, what you want in life, and what you bring to the table. You must understand your negotiables and nonnegotiables. Lastly, you must be emotionally and psychologically available to even consider being in a relationship. You cannot be involved with anyone else. Never be okay with just hooking up or trying someone out.

If you're available in every sense of the word and you meet someone, be sure to take the time to get to know that person and see if he or she is what you want. Being open to starting a relationship will allow you to see others that you may be interested in for who they are, and you will also allow them to see you for who you are. If something goes wrong in a new relationship, because you were not involved with anyone else, you won't decide immediately to fall back on the person you put on the back burner (a secondary person you are holding on to as a friend). This is why it's very important to be emotionally available and not attached to anyone else when you begin a relationship.

Unfortunately, people often hook up or get caught up in relationships because they temporarily satisfy their fleshly desires, but if the other parties get emotionally attached to them, they could end up in considerable pain. Don't start a relationship with someone you have no interest in having a long-term relationship with.

Hooking up with or just trying someone out opens you up to all sorts of possible long-term issues such as sexually transmitted infections (STIs), unwanted pregnancies, psychological issues, stalkers, negative spiritual experiences, and so much more. Hooking up has caused many people pain and to end up thinking no good men or women exist.

Many good men and women are not given the opportunity they deserve to show their goodness. Singleness has been made more complicated than it should be. Many of us are single for a variety of reasons good and bad. Some reasons could be geographic location, personal interests, beliefs, compatibility, past hurts, and baggage from one or more relationships. Some are single because they are not up-front or honest about their feelings or what they want. Some play games and are not respectful of one another; some try to change others, and so many more reasons. Playing games causes frustration and leads to a person forming negative beliefs. Worst of all, it leads to a situation where one person is playing games with others' emotions or simply do not know what they want; that will always end up with someone getting hurt.

Some people are not willing to get out and meet others at bars, clubs, or even at church. Different people can have differing expectations. Single people's limited geographical situations can make it hard for them to meet people interested in a relationship. In this situation, it does help when friends suggest connections they can make with others or if they try online dating sites.

Those who are willing to get out there can become overwhelmed when they meet too many people, and I'm one of them. Going out and being approached by multiple guys can be stressful. A couple of times, I placed myself on different dating sites and was flooded with messages and requests. In less than twenty-four hours, I deleted my accounts. At other times, friends wanted to introduce me to men friends of theirs, but I'd ask myself, *What if it doesn't work?* I wouldn't want to ruin the friendship or make it awkward. As a result, I declined those opportunities to meet people. As you become wiser and have less tolerance, it becomes more challenging to waste time or deal with foolishness.

A person's beliefs stemming from cultural or religious constraints may be a reason he or she is single, and many consider their cultures or religious beliefs to be very important and nonnegotiable. In an era when difference is not celebrated, we must defy the norm. It is important to respect others' values, religion, and family culture. These are the foundations of inner beliefs. We must learn to spread love and respect.

People's interests or beliefs or their compatibility with other people can be other reasons they're single. Opposites certainly attract, but some people who want to respect their cultural or religious backgrounds are looking for someone from the same cultural or religious backgrounds.

Some people are single because they're carrying around baggage from past relationships that ended badly. Their past partners might have played games with their hearts, a very cruel thing to do. Why play games? Be honest. If you don't want to be with someone, tell him or her. Why have sexual relations with someone if you have no intention of marrying him or her? Why form soul ties? Doing so is selfish and inconsiderate.

Some people say that it takes time to get to know someone and you never know what the future holds. When you're still getting to know someone, you might not yet know if a relationship is on the horizon. But if that's the case, why become physically intimate? Physical intimacy should be reserved for the one you will say, "I do" to.

Many have dated or even gotten engaged, lived as if they were going to get married, and given of themselves but marriage never happened. Being intimately involved with someone but then being rejected by that person can fill you with bitterness and anger, and that's not worth it. I can testify to the emotional turmoil and resentment that can build up and have a negative impact on your personality. The number of singles carrying around emotional pain is unimaginable. Unwanted pregnancy is also a risk. Some will say, "But I use a contraceptive!" but contraceptives can fail, and contraceptives cannot save you from emotional and spiritual damage.

Many people are in a relationship they describe as complicated, and relationships can become complicated by sexual involvement, a lack of commitment, no plans to marry, and dishonesty on one or both sides. What is the real purpose of such a relationship? What do people in complicated relationships expect from each other in the long run? Do they know each other's expectations and desires? Are they proud of and satisfied by their limited relationship?

Be honest and evaluate your status; are you in a relationship that allows you to introduce your significant other to your friends and say,

"This is my mate"? If you cannot, it may be time to reconsider if you are actually in a relationship. You are more valuable than a temporary solution for someone who's looking only for a quick fix.

There are many good men and women in this world. You have to be open enough to see people for who they are, and you have to first know and love yourself. Figure out why or what is causing you to be single. Tell yourself that good men and women do exist. Look closely at your expectations of people. Do you know the type of person you would like to be with? Are your expectations realistic? Are you getting out and exploring your area? It's fine to get out and do things on your own. If your beliefs and culture are important to you, are you getting involved in cultural or religious activities such as volunteering? Don't get involved in one of those "It's complicated" relationships because they will keep you single or get you involved in the wrong relationships.

If you're carrying around pain caused by failed relationships, realize that you are not alone. There is nothing you could say or do that someone else has not said or done, so stop being hard on yourself; we've all made choices we later wish we hadn't. Let go of your baggage and remember that every experience good or bad can be a learning experience.

Prayer

God, thank you for continuing to help me grow. Thank you for opening my eyes to my negative ways and helping me face myself. Help me to heal my deep wounds and free myself of all my baggage and bondage. I am no longer willing to keep myself hostage for things done in my youth or in my state of unknowing. Now that I know better, I will do better. Help me to be free! I pray a blessing over all those who need healing and freedom.

Thank you for the good men and women who still stand on their values. Bless them for doing the right thing and treating others the right way. I give you glory for the victory that I know I will receive. In Jesus Christ's name I pray, amen.

CHAPTER 4

Let's Just Have Sex

Friends with benefits? Let's be honest. How many people are really just friends with benefits? If you have a friend with benefits, you're lying to yourself and heading down a road of soul ties, hurt, and possible resentment. At least one of you is playing along thinking that the other will eventually change his or her mind and commit to a real relationship. In the meantime, you two play the game.

Sometimes, people who are friends with benefits end up in temporary relationships, but the majority of the time, one of them ends up emotionally devastated and takes it out on others. How many people single or married do you know who are angry, bitter, and always making negative comments about relationships? That could have been caused by a history of being in uncommitted relationships or emotional baggage.

Sex is very beautiful in marriage because there is no shame, guilt, or worry about anything. Unfortunately, sexual involvement outside marriage can cause the worst pains, situations, complications, and long-lasting negative effects. Some may admit or recognize that they were on an emotional roller-coaster wondering if such a relationship was forever or temporary, but what sort of life is that? No one deserves to wonder, *How long will this last? Will my friend with benefits feel the need to try someone else?*

You may have asked yourself, *Why am I single? What am I doing wrong?* If you are being physically intimate with someone outside marriage, that might be why you're single. Yes, we all have sexual desires, but sex isn't a pastime or hobby, and outside of marriage, it can result in hurt and emotional baggage you'll drag into your next relationship. It's definitely better to be single and celibate than to be in a relationship that began because of lust and ended up being miserable.

How many people do you know have relationships that began with casual sex? In some cases, one person feels stuck in a relationship he or she never really wanted to be in. At other times, the two people just settle and stay together even if they really don't want to be in a relationship with each other. Such relationships are not healthy or fulfilling.

Imagine the stress, headaches, and emotional turmoil that come with being sexually involved with someone who you think might not commit to or profess his or her love for you. Being single and not involved sexually with anyone is much better than risking being hurt when a purely sexual relationship collapses. I'll take singleness and celibacy any day over hurt, an "It's complicated" relationship, or being strung along only to become bitter and hateful.

Some people may ask, "How is it being selfish to have casual sex? We're consenting adults." Some people fail to see how thinking only about themselves is wrong and could inflict major emotional pain or psychological trauma on someone. If consenting adults love and care for each other, why don't they get married? Why would consenting adults be in it just for the sex? Is anyone expecting a relationship at some point? You might be surprised by the answers to these questions.

Both parties might be consenting adults, but they'll likely have differing expectations. Often, they will just go along with the relationship without asking themselves, *What's our purpose? Are we kicking it with a purpose or just going with the flow?* Unfortunately, when people are just kicking it or going with the flow, one person might think, *We're in an unspoken relationship* while the other one thinks, *I can still do what I want with other people because we're not committed.* That disconnect can end up hurting one or both parties.

It's important to be clear about your expectations and know the other person's expectations; that way, neither of you will be misled. A lot of people are single but are also in an it's complicated–type relationship. No, it's not complicated—it's simple. Someone is playing along hoping the other will commit. It's not complicated: you're either in a relationship or you're not.

When we don't think about how our actions can negatively impact others, we're not thinking long term, and this is why some people can snap at exes. Playing games or misleading someone in a relationship may work for a time, but eventually, someone will get hurt. Unfortunately, many people sleep with others assuming they are in an exclusive relationship while the other thinks it's just a casual thing. Many do not see anything wrong with sleeping around, but that's morally wrong and negatively impactful in many ways. It could cause a lot of suffering for others who want a real relationship.

Take some time and reflect about your status. Think about your previous relationships. Instead of passing judgment on anyone for snapping or having baggage, ask yourself if you have ever hurt others by misleading them and haven't developed an adult mind-set. The older one becomes, the more mature and disciplined one is supposed to be. Unfortunately, there are many people not being disciplined and continue with infidelity and games.

I don't understand those who think only about their own desires. I would rather be celibate than lie to myself and someone else simply to please my body. Wasting time with temporary gratification is just not worth it. Why waste time by playing games and risk hurting others? Physical intimacy is beautiful and sacred, and it should be shared only in marriage—a husband and wife willing to grow with each other.

We must think about the effect our actions will have in the long as well as the short term. Unfortunately, people get themselves into relationships that are toxic and get upset when they end up hurt. At times, people settle for others who cause them constant emotional, psychological, and or even physical pain. Others connect with people for sexual or financial reasons and have no interest in long-term relationships. A worse situation is when a person with very low self-esteem connects with someone who is controlling and abusive. All of these are the wrong reasons to be involved with someone. Being single is not that bad when you heal yourself emotionally and spiritually. It is better to be alone and celibate than to risk pain that could turn your heart bitter and angry.

It is a sad scenario when people claim others are hurting them but they are in fact the ones hurting others. These people may be allowing the pain or bitterness from previous relationships to perpetuate and hurt new people who come into their lives. Be careful how you treat people; what goes around comes around. Beware that our hearts can cause us to act foolishly and not think logically. As a result, our choices can be self-endangering, and we will choose to be with a person who hurts us, causing us more pain.

Some people hold out for a certain person or type of person and don't even see the people around them who would like to enter a relationship with them. They may lie to themselves and think, *I'm not ready* or *There are no good men or women out there*. How many of you were or are like that? Can you see how being in a friend with benefits relationship kept you from being available for the right person? I'm not passing judgment on you here; I used to be the queen of excuses.

I want to offer you my perspective on being at peace with being single if that's your situation. It is helpful to have different perspectives so you can make a decision that is good for you. Hopefully, the perspective I provide will help in your search for a true relationship if that's your desire. Casual sex may satisfy the flesh temporarily, but it is ultimately a selfish act. Sex is not just an act; it involves more and should be enjoyed by two people who love and are committed to each other. Don't let the world's simplistic view fool you of the beauty that is involved in the act.

We all make mistakes, but we should learn from them and strive to become better people. When we improve ourselves, we influence those around us. Let us strive to do better so less people will be traumatized due to the lack of commitment and our temporary sexual pleasure. We should encourage the young and those who are not married to practice celibacy and heal their hearts and minds while they wait for their king or queen to marry.

Prayer

God, you created me and know the sexual desires you have placed in me. Please help me to be disciplined and wait for the mate you have created just for me. And when that time comes, may I be fulfilled in pleasing my mate as much as my mate will be fulfilled in pleasing me. I claim the victory and wait patiently for you to answer my prayer.

But since sexual immorality is occurring, each man should have sexual relations with his own wife, and each woman with her own husband. (1 Corinthians 7:2 NIV)

Marriage should be honored by all, and the marriage bed kept pure, for God will judge the adulterer and all the sexually immoral. (Hebrews 13:4 NIV)

CHAPTER 5

Am I the Only One Struggling?

Are you the only one struggling? Are you the only single person feeling alone? Are you the only one feeling like you'll never find your one true love? No. Millions of single people are pondering those questions right now. Some might be at a club, a church service, at home watching a movie, at a gym, with family, or attending a function to distract their minds from their daily issues. You're not alone. The real question is how you'll handle being single.

You're not the only single person desiring companionship and intimate relations. There are times when these feelings will be strong, and other times, you will be tempted to settle for anybody so you can have that companionship. Don't settle because the desires pass. Being single can be a very emotional roller-coaster ride.

During special times of the year or on certain occasions when you feel the sting of loneliness, be careful. Don't drink too much, hook up with someone, curse someone out, or exhibit negative behavior. If you must, lock yourself up and turn off your phone. You might feel that you're in a deep hole you can't get yourself out of, but that feeling won't last. Do something positive instead, to help yourself overcome the sting of loneliness.

Get out, get some air, go to the gym, or go for a walk and take in the beauty of nature. Find something to do that will keep you from creating a mess you'll have to apologize for. I've had to do my share of apologizing for negative behavior because I didn't listen to my instincts.

I should have recognized that I was not in a good place and needed to stay home.

People don't forget what you do if it's way out of character; if you do something negative, apologize for it. The mistakes I've made in that regard taught me to be humble and not judge anyone because I can't be sure I have that person's whole story.

You might face emotional challenges when you're around couples or married folks and think everyone is happy. You may even long for what they have. What people don't tell you is that some of them may have just had an argument and are putting on a show. Others may be happy and have learned to help each other cope during hard times. You don't know what's really going on in people's lives and you should never covet someone else's life.

Instead of coveting other people's relationships, pray that they are happy, are fulfilling and will grow old with each other. Couples, especially those who are married, need prayer and support because the world makes it very challenging for them to stay happily married. Everyone will have some sort of struggle and deserve to be happy.

There will also be many days when you are grateful for your singleness and the lack of problems caused by relationships. How many times have you seen or heard couples fighting and thought, *Thank God I'm single. I don't have time for that nonsense*? If you won't admit it, I will. There have been many times when I have thought, *Yup, this is why I am single!* Relationship conflicts are so uncomfortable. There are times when you will appreciate your singleness, especially after such example: you start dating someone and think, *This person is it! I love everything about him/her!* Then, they stop being consistent and seemed bothered when you contact them. You start to feel as if you have done something wrong but discover he or she is pursuing multiple people. One day you are it, the next day you're not. Your emotions are all over the place, you're angry and annoyed. Slowly, you find yourself returning to the negative way of thinking that no good men or women are out there. The truth is you didn't do anything wrong; it was the person that became inconsistent and chose to pursue multiple people. There are plenty of good men and women out in the world; the individual you're dealing with is the issue. This person is unsure of what he/she wants or has a view of relationships that differs from yours. Don't beat yourself up. Reflect, analyze, and evaluate the situation rather than going back to that negative mind-set that once kept you in bondage. Don't let someone's immaturity or undisciplined mannerisms take you to a bitter place—stay free.

It's hard to free yourself of anger and bitterness, but you need to if you want to find peace. You must find love within and remind yourself; *I'm loved and special, and it's okay to move on if the other person cannot appreciate me.* Remind yourself that your mate is out there alone and growing into the best version of himself or herself for you. There's no need to stress or worry. Be patient even if you're not patient by nature; patience is a virtue. You have free will and can choose to hold onto or let go of bitterness and anger. What is meant for you will be for you, and no matter what you do, you cannot mess it up. You just have to be patient, continue working on yourself, and wait on God.

Have faith and live life to the fullest in peace, joy, and love. Don't be afraid to open yourself up to others. Find yourself by determining exactly what you like and don't like, and figure out the things you want, but don't get involved sexually with anyone. Sex complicates things, and if you do not get a commitment, you may find yourself going to a place of anger, which will steal your joy and peace.

Take your time of singleness and feeling lonely to do the things you've always wanted to do. Do everything your heart desires without constraints; try out a new sport, activity, or hobby. Strive to be a positive light, a force of goodness, peace, joy, and love. In a world full of darkness, hurt, bitterness, and anger, do something positive. You are free to do whatever your heart desires. You can volunteer to help the sick, disabled, elderly or displaced veterans. You can help to bring a smile on the faces of others.

You can make a difference in this respect if you are healthy in mind, body, and soul. You are a shining light; you are not alone on this journey of singleness. Someone else has experienced everything you have. Instead of dwelling or focusing on your feelings of emptiness, fill yourself with love, peace, joy and laughter with things you like to do.

Don't be afraid to go out and explore all that this world has to offer. Pray or send out positive energy, love, and joy to others, and thank God for how you are growing and finding a deeper level of peace each day. Be positive and share a smile with all those around. We are free to be a beacon of light and joy everywhere we go and in everything we do.

Prayer

I am struggling, God. Help me during this time. I am learning that others are going through similar battles but help me to control my emotions. I am not perfect, and I need You, amen.

??

CHAPTER 6

Challenges We Face

Being single does have its challenges but also blessings. It's up to you to find the good in your singleness. Most of us were created to be in fellowship with another human being; however, some people were meant to be alone and will never have an issue with their singleness. Which category are you in?

I know I'm meant to be in a relationship. Some people have questioned it, it's just that I'm very selective. If being single is hard for you and you don't enjoy being alone, you'll have to do some soul searching and cleansing. Another person will be able to bring only temporary joy and peace; long-lasting peace and joy must come from within.

Let's talk about some of the serious struggles you might be having as a single person. The struggles are very real and can be challenging. There are times when you want to be held, caressed, kissed on, and made love to. If you are a virgin, you may not understand these desires, but that's actually the best thing for you. It's better not to understand or be able to relate to those desires than to have the additional baggage of having had more than one sexual partner. If you are a virgin, keep your virtue and do not compromise yourself. Save yourself from all of the unnecessary baggage that comes from dealing with multiple partners.

Other times, single people just want to watch a movie and cuddle with someone; or have someone they can talk to or vent with. Having another human being present so you can mentally release is a blessing.

Single people might want someone to handle areas of their lives in which they do not feel strong such as finances or certain chores. Even if you are a self-sufficient person, it can be even better when you have someone you trust, love, and feel safe with who is willing to share the load of different things in your life. An example would be that some people are great at cooking but not cleaning and their partner is great at cleaning but not cooking. The two people balance each other. One of the biggest benefits of a relationship is hearing someone say, "Hey babe, I'm going to take care of this for you" or "Do you want me to cook tonight?" That emphasizes the fact that they're not alone. Most people enjoy having someone do something nice for them.

But don't get me wrong here—it's better to be single than to settle for a miserable relationship, so don't settle. Being single has its good and bad moments, and if you learn strategies to better deal with your singleness, you can find peace and joy.

Dealing with unmet desires for physical intimacy can be one of the hardest parts of being single, and it is the reason many singles end up settling. This is where self-discipline and control are required. It doesn't help that society and the media glorify casual sex or sex outside marriage. I am not passing judgment on anyone for what they have done or are doing because I have my own issues and have created my share of personal messes. For the majority of the years since my divorce, I've been single and abstaining, but that hasn't been easy.

Being single is not a curse but simply a season of life. Some people are single by choice while others are made single through a breakup, divorce, or death. Being single might seem to be the end of the world, but it is not; you'll get through it. If I can be single and enjoy life, so can you. In spite of my challenges, I'm still standing and have found peace in the single state. Some days, the peace may flee leaving me feeling defeated, but I get to work occupying my mind with other matters. I'm grateful that those times usually don't last long though they seem they will last forever; I eventually regain my peace. No pain lasts forever. You have to go through the process but keep your head up and remember this is only a season.

In addition to glorifying casual sex, society and the media portray single people negatively in so many ways. Do you recognize some of these examples? *Single people are wild, have no self-respect, are cheaters, date multiple people at a time, they are full of drama and need to experiment with a person sexually before committing.* Trying people out should not even be a consideration. If you're considering someone for a relationship, ask yourself, *Who is this person? Does he (or she) have the qualities I'm looking for in a mate? Will she (or he) support me in the bad as well as the good times? Will he (or she) accept me while we help each other grow?* The answers to these questions can take time to determine; you cannot rely on just what a person tells you; you have to also watch his or her behavior. If it doesn't align with his or her words, the answer to these questions is *no*.

Don't fall for the negative portrayal of singles. The media can negatively impact people who are trying to have wholesome relationships. All forms of media are entertainment, not a way of life. Casual sex is not the way to go. As I mentioned, there's nothing wrong with staying single if you're not defiling others sexually, being a manipulator, player, or leading others on. Being single is a journey of enjoying yourself alone and spending time with those you love—family and close friends usually of the same sex.

Society's negative portrayal of singles makes it difficult for all singles. I don't like to watch movies involving singles. It's a struggle to live the single life, and it's made worse by seeing singles' foolishness on TV. It's even more annoying when media present the idea that it's okay to sleep around with as many people as you want, that singles are homewreckers, people who are willing to take others' mates, and people enjoying being a sidepiece or a mistress. I don't like leftovers or someone else's mess. I don't want any part of someone who is dating someone, engaged, or married; why would someone who was unfaithful to someone else ever be faithful to anyone? Have you ever heard the saying? *How you get them is how you will lose them.* Ask the questions in the beginning and stand on your morals and values.

Show everyone that single people have values, respect relationships and can live their own lives. Don't do anything that could bring you pain just because you want to do what everyone else does. Yes, you'll have some hard, sad, frustrating, and lonely days and nights, but during those times, don't fall into a trap that can have a lasting negative impact on you. Instead, keep yourself busy. Be on guard for temptations and know what you want. I pray you find peace so when the time comes for you to be in a relationship that is meant for you, you'll end up in a healthy, loving, godly relationship with someone who will adore you for you.

Everyone is different in regard to beliefs, upbringing, customs, culture, and values. No one will do things exactly the way you do. Despite the challenges of being single, ask yourself, *Why is this so hard for me? What's the lesson I need to learn or thing I must do during this time? What can I do to enjoy myself and be a light for the world?*

How are you going to be a light and maintain your peace? Most people feel a need for physical or intimate relations because of our human nature, but that's no reason to settle for or get involved with someone. Be careful about what you do and how you treat others. Always treat others the way you would want to be treated.

Prayer

God, these challenges can be very difficult. At times, I want to settle and not care, but I know that's not what you want for me. Help me always remember my value and the purpose you have for me. Guide my steps and show me what I need to do to comfort myself. I pray for all those who are in the same situation I'm in, and I ask you to help them overcome their trials. Help us all to not fall into temptation or hurt anyone. Give me strength and guide my steps in Jesus Christ's name I pray, amen.

CHAPTER 7

Real Talk about Singleness

Is being single really that bad? Your perception of being single and how you allow others to make you feel will determine the outcome of your experience. At one time, I believed something was wrong with me for being single. I was influenced by what people told me about being single. Here are a few statements that have been made to me.

"You're too beautiful to be alone. What's wrong with you?"

"You must be very hard to get along with."

"It's a shame to see you waste away!"

"You need to change your ways so you can get a man."

Such statements led me to believe there was something wrong with me when in fact there was nothing wrong with me—I just have certain expectations and standards. Despite my standards and expectations, I have always been and will always be a work in progress. Who isn't? I won't deny that I needed to work on some issues; I was holding onto some hurts, and I'd made up excuses whenever a guy was interested in me. It has taken me time to move forward. Again, who doesn't have things they must work through?

As I matured and learned about myself, I became able to set expectations for relationships because I knew what I was willing to do for and give to a man, and that allowed me to view some potential relationships with real clarity. I ran across some men who wanted to toy with me, who wanted to stay friends with exes, who wanted me to be a friend with benefits, and expected me to settle for that.

Hmmm … I'm supposed to give the best of me to a man who wants to give me only a part of himself because he's not willing to let go of people with whom he has been sexually involved with? Why would I ever want to give my all to such a man? Let's think logically and analyze the situation. If I'm devoting time and attention to a man, wouldn't it be respectful for him to demonstrate the same level of respect and attention? Would it truly make sense for me to accept pieces when I am giving a whole? Entertaining multiple people distracts from truly getting to know a person and provides an excuse to not make a relationship work.

At one time, I entertained multiple people at the same time and was not looking for any sort of relationship with them. It was a stressful juggling act, and I'll never do that again. Plus, I've matured and realized how foolish my actions were. Those who are honest with themselves know that being involved with multiple people makes it a challenge to be honest with your feelings about anyone. Some would say, "Women do it all the time!" "Yes, you can date multiple people," "There are ways to do it," "Dating several people is fine!" and so on. Some people will always justify their actions even if it is wrong. I know not everyone will agree with me and it is fine. I've seen and known people who made decisions that they thought were best while dating multiple people and end up regretting those decision. People have told me that they made decisions when they were in their feelings or didn't give the other person a fair chance due to anger or fear. No one gets a fair chance when you're involved with multiple people. All you can fulfill in that situation is your illogical fleshly desires. Base your major decisions about relationships on prayer, logic, rationality, instinct, and then flesh.

You know that people can put on temporary shows for you or act a certain way for a period of time before their true selves emerge. You don't want to make a hasty decision about someone who is capable of doing that, watch his or her true self emerge, and find yourself stuck. Take time to get to know someone, pray, make logical decisions, and pay close attention to the person's behavior.

Think back to a time you were interested in someone with whom things were going well; you two were getting along just fine. Then, all of a sudden, the calls or texts stopped coming, he or she started complaining about being constantly busy and became agitated when you disagreed with him or her. Your emotions were all over the place, right? You wondered what had gone wrong. Then you found out that someone else had entered the picture, how did you feel? If you could go back in time, would you still entertain that person knowing you were about to get on an emotional roller-coaster?

Let's turn the tables here. Let's say you're interested in one person, and things are going well for the two of you until you're introduced to someone else or an old flame comes knocking. You decide just to call and text him or her, but that cuts down on your contact with the person you're currently involved with; your focus shifts. Your current gets upset by your lack of attention, and you become the one making excuses; you feel he or she is becoming clingy, demanding, annoying, stifling ... You may end things with him or her for that reason when in reality, you're the one who has become someone else. He or she opened up to you and started trusting you, but you betrayed that trust, and he or she ends up hurt and distrustful of you and perhaps people in his or her future.

All this negativity came about simply because you wanted to try someone else out and was not mature or disciplined to reject the temptation and allow things to evolve or end with your current person. If you had been mature and disciplined and knew what you wanted, you would have never considered someone else while still trying to determine what may or may not happen with the current person in a respectful way. Changing on a person because of a third party will always lead to someone experiencing emotional pain. Emotional pain inflicted because a negative cycle of *hurt people hurting people*.

Many people think, *I'm going to just do me and get what I want* without considering the emotional damage they can inflict on others, who end up shying away from future relationships because they want to avoid repeating the pain caused by someone who was not honest with them. They end up wanting to protect themselves by not opening up to others.

In other situations, people will say they aren't interested, but their actions contradict that; they're actually messing around with other people. Those who are honest about not wanting to start up anything with you and telling you that they are involved with someone else is sending respect your way.

Let our words and actions be in alignment. It's unfortunate that we can make up excuses to justify our wrongs, our lack of self-discipline, and the hurt we have caused others. The minute you decide to entertain, hook up with, or get involved with another human being, you take on a responsibility for his or her heart and relational mind-set. And it works the other way around as well. This is why it's important during your season of singleness to ask yourself some questions: *Where am I in this stage of my life? Am I ready to be in a relationship?* No matter how sexual you are or the desires you have, during your time as a single, you must exercise self-discipline and know that you take on a responsibility for someone when you get into a relationship with that person.

Actions and words must align when dealing with other people and their hearts. It is not often people want to have real talk about singleness. Instead, people like to judge, ridicule or make false assumptions. Dealing with multiple people causes confusion and always leads to multiple people getting hurt. Any decisions made about relationships should be based on prayer, logic, rationale, instinct, and flesh. Be sure to watch the person's long-term behaviors. Be logical and think about your actions and do not justify any selfish act. Not everyone will have the same expectations you do or be able to deal with situations the same way you do; their different backgrounds and experiences will come into play. Some people are more sensitive than others, and your actions can be more detrimental to them. Be careful with your actions and words.

Prayer

God, help me be logical, not selfish, when I come across someone who attracts me. Help me think about my life and help me appreciate those who care about me. Help me remove any selfish ways in me and be grateful for those who love me. Help me to know that if I am blessed with a good thing, I do not need to keep looking for something else because I know the grass is not greener on the other side. Help me be disciplined and able to reciprocate the love given to me. In your name I pray.

Profession

I speak life over my life! I am disciplined and able to love another. I am full of peace, joy, and contentment. I respect and love God, who is blessing me. I am loving and able to reciprocate all the love and support I receive.

CHAPTER 8

What People Won't Talk About

This section of my book is not based on research but on my observations of people and society and my experiences. I hope my testimony will help you grow and heal. During your healing process, you might want to seek guidance from a therapist or member of the clergy to assist you in your healing and growing process.

Let's talk about the relational mind-set, the way a person thinks about relationships is based on their experiences with them. We change or form mind-sets based on our interactions with others. Our relational mind-sets may be good, positive, negative, or even destructive, but they constantly evolve especially when we become interested in dating. So, we have to be careful to not damage others' relational mind-sets.

The best way to do that is to first know who you are and what you want in another person. You have no business being involved with anyone until you figure that out. Just going through the motions of a relationship is not a responsible or respectful way to deal with others; that can hurt and lead them to wonder what was wrong with them. Everyone's heart and mind are precious and should not be played with.

Think of a time you were hurt badly; how did that affect your mind and heart? Anyone who says, "I didn't care" or "I've never been hurt," is lying. Everyone has been hurt in some way, but not everyone deals with that hurt in the same way. In some cases, people can be so hurt that the love or affection they feel for someone becomes hate—a very sad outcome. They gave someone their love and expected it to be reciprocated, but it wasn't. When love is not reciprocated the heart will be broken. A broken heart can lead to many different reactions.

Many relationships have been destroyed when a third party came into the picture even if it was not sexually; it could have been an intellectual connection or attraction. The one who suffers may start feeling resentful and that can lead to his or her hating the one that inflicted the pain. Unfortunately, no one really knows how pain and suffering will cause them to react.

We can change our feelings of bitterness, anger, and resentment if we first become aware of those feelings and then decide we want to exchange them for positive feelings. A lot of men and women are walking around broken and bitter because no one has ever helped them realize that their negative feelings were destroying them. Sometimes, all it takes for them to heal is for someone to recognize their hurt and help them forgive and overcome that pain, but many people don't want to get involved with angry and bitter people. As a result, those who are hurt and bitter pass on their pain to others, who end up doing the same to others—on and on.

I was that angry and bitter person at one time, but I've healed and daily I work on protecting my heart and mind. I hope that this book will help those who are broken to begin the journey to self-healing and peace.

Entertaining More Than One Person

I talked about this briefly earlier, but I want to go into a little more detail about it. I've seen and spoken to so many people who believe that nonmonogamy or dating multiple people was the main cause of their relationships not working out or why they continued to have issues with relationships.

There are times for emotions and other times for logic. Can you really talk to or entertain more than one person at a time? Logically, no. I challenge those who disagree with that to consider their relationships and ask themselves, *Am I in a great, lasting relationship? How long have my relationships lasted?* I'll wait for them to try to rationalize why none of their relationships have worked out and how that was always the other person's fault.

We should be honest with ourselves about why our relationships have not worked out. Relationships are never perfect, nor is being single, but we shouldn't allow society to lie to us about relationships and singleness. If you are in a relationship that you want out of, be honest with the other party about that; don't just disappear or stop calling him or her without explaining that you want to break things off. Show him or her respect, and you will be amazed at how much more life will bless you.

Watching shows about relationships, people cheating, and people snapping could make you paranoid and think that everyone out there dating is crazy with a capital *C*. Such shows could make you feel hopeless about finding true love or someone who is honest and faithful, so disregard them. You can find the many good women and men out there if you know what you want and the type of person you would like to grow old with.

Dating multiple people works only if you compromise your beliefs or yourself; don't do that, and don't settle for someone who does. That will just cause pain that, as I've mentioned, can be perpetuated far beyond the people directly involved. It's hard enough to deal with and satisfy one person—why would you want to create chaos by playing around with multiple people's hearts and minds? This is a recipe for disaster, and too many people have gotten killed, hurt, or imprisoned for this foolishness, which is simply not worth it.

People were not created to have multiple partners. That creates conflicts even in polygamous societies and particularly when children come along. Hurt people teach children hate, bitterness, and anger and how to blame others, not care about the mind-set or emotions of others, and think only of themselves. There are exceptions; some parents lead moral and ethical lives but have children who don't learn those lessons; children are unpredictable, but their parents have the responsibility to teach and show their children how to treat others with empathy and respect by modeling it themselves.

Children—and that includes you when you were a child—don't come with a user's manual. If you were mistreated or slighted when you were growing up, let that go. The adults in your life probably did the best they could raising you with the knowledge and experience they had. If they pained you, you can heal yourself. If needed, get counseling, which is never a bad thing (just take the time to find the right counselor for you). As long as there is anger and bitterness in your heart, you won't be able to experience peace and love. It's important to heal, let go, and forgive so you can move on and become happy.

I tried putting my children in a bubble to protect them from being exposed to terrible things, but that's not possible. Parents must make sure that their behavior models how healthy relationships work, and that means relationships involving only two people.

The long-term negative effect of people attempting to be in relationships with numerous people is that many end up hurt, damaged, and bitter whether they get married or remain single. It's a vicious cycle of pain breathing pain, hurt breathing hurt, and bitterness breathing bitterness. The cycle of bitterness that can be created by broken relationships will end only when people realize the value of others' hearts and minds. Our children will learn from what we do and say, and we can teach them how to not hurt others and how not to be hurt by others. I hope to teach as many singles, young and old, to respect others and not play the foolish games that have caused generations of hurt and created a society with so many relational and mental issues. Let's start by creating a different image in our minds of beauty, peace, joy and love in our state of singleness. Create an image of being completely devoted to one person that treats you like royalty and you are able to reciprocate every emotion and action.

I'm Just Going to Have Sex

We all know people who were not interested in relationships but just sex. Are they happy? Are they on a roller-coaster ride? I've been in that situation myself, and it was horrible. People looking just for sex can lie to themselves and try to believe they are in a relationship, but they aren't. Sex will do that to you; it'll have you believing the sky is green when it's clearly blue. A couple of hot nights of sex is not healthy for your emotions or psyche not to mention your health considering the prevalence of STIs and the possibility of pregnancy even if you're using contraceptives.

Sex involves an exchange of many things other than just bodily fluids; you are forming and taking on a part of the other person. Casual sex tends to attract negative consequences; it can damage your soul and affect your heart and brain, and it's just not worth that. The older I become, the more peace, love and joy I seek to have in my life.

Sex is wonderful in the right context. Animals can have sex without emotional connections, but we humans need more than that; we need commitment. Many monogamous men and women would not even consider it any other way, and for that reason, they don't trivialize sex.

Sex is one of the most sacred and beautiful acts you can enjoy with another person in marriage, but with some people, it has devolved into simply a way to self-gratify, and that can lead to unwanted pregnancies and destroyed relationships and cause people to commit unthinkable acts that destroy souls and hearts. Think of the pain left in the hearts of women who have terminated their pregnancies or had to give up their infants in adoption.

Consider the blood that has been shed, the hearts that have been destroyed, and the minds that have become unstable because of the spiritual hurt caused by casual sex. I am not condemning anyone who has been in a negative situation resulting in casual sex that has led to something else; I'm simply bringing to light the possible consequences people should be aware of.

Before you have sex with someone outside of marriage, ask yourself if it is worth the risks involved, if this is someone you want to be tied to for the rest of your life if you produce a child. How much do you know about this person? How did you reach the point that you want to have sex with him or her? Everything's a choice, and your choices shouldn't end up hurting you or anyone else.

To avoid negatively affecting others, we should have those difficult conversations with them. It's always easier not to, but we won't resolve anything, and that might make a bad situation worse. Peace and joy come from knowing that we aren't inflicting pain on others and that our minds are free of guilt, shame, pain, anger, and disappointment. We have to monitor our actions because they cause positive or negative reactions.

No matter how flattering it may seem to have multiple people interested in you, be respectful of yourself and them. Be mature and have the challenging conversations when you don't want to be with someone, so you don't leave him or her wondering what happened when you cut them off.

Before you tell yourself that having sex is no big deal, determine if your intended partner is someone who would be willing to wait for the two of you to develop your relationship, if your relationship would survive if you could not have sex, and if he or she would be loyal to you if you lost everything. The choices you make can grant you freedom and peace and help you not cause unnecessary emotional and psychological harm to anyone.

Prayer

Father, I come before you and ask for help. You know the situations I am in. I want to free myself from anything that is not good for me. Help me see the areas I need to improve in. Protect my heart and the hearts of those whom I might have affected negatively. Give me strength to make better choices moving forward. Be with me and forgive all my errors.

？

CHAPTER 9

It's Better to Wait Than Jump In and Become Worse Off

I'm sure you've heard that it's important to be in a relationship, that you shouldn't wait too long to get married or have children, and that you should just have sex with someone so you can get over another person, but I'm going to contradict all that.

Don't make the mistake of getting involved with a person just because you want to be in a relationship or are trying to get over someone. Make sure you are ready for the relationship and can verbalize your desires. If you've never thought about what you want out of life or a relationship, you may not know what you want. You may not even know what type of person you want to attract other than a good looking or pretty person. Looks don't last forever. Gravity will always have its way with bodies, faces, and hair. Will you abandon your loved one if they end up sick, with dementia, or unable to satisfy you sexually? Make sure you are ready for that relationship. It is always better to wait than to jump into something you are not ready to entertain.

It took me a while to figure out that I needed someone I could talk to about anything, someone who would make me feel safe emotionally and physically and be willing to do nice things for me without asking. Mutual loyalty and honesty are also important to me. I don't believe in competing for someone's affection or attention; I consider that silly. How can two people compete for a person's attention or affection when each person is different? Everyone is different in so many ways. Plus, if you have to compete for someone's attention, it may be likely that the person doesn't have your best interests at heart. A person who truly cares about you will never make you feel you have to compete with others for him or her. Beware of the feeling that you have to do extra to get or keep someone's attention.

Waiting patiently is important. Everything takes time to discover; you have to be open to life's possibilities, but don't jump out of the pan, a bad relationship, into the fire, a worse one. Know what you're getting into before you get into it.

As you wait, deal with your hurts, remove any negatives, and plan for a positive future. Cleanse yourself of your soul ties, the emotional connections with people you had sexual or other relationships with from the past. Soul ties keep you connected and unable to fully move forward. To move forward into a happy and healthy relationship you must be free of any soul ties. Learn to set healthy boundaries with people to take care of yourself and your relationships.

During my season of being single, I realized that loyalty was very important to me. If I had to compete with anything but God in a relationship, I would be unhappy. A man might have children or responsibilities, but that would not be an issue for me. What would be an issue is if a man disrespected or allowed others to disrespect me. Worst is if he felt the need to entertain other women while being involved with me. Loyalty and respect are my nonnegotiables. Everyone has nonnegotiables; have you identified yours?

During this period of healing, as you get to know yourself and what you want, your emotions may become challenging and prompt you to just jump into a relationship, but that would be quitting in the middle of your progress. On your most challenging days, the greatest temptations will come your way. Stand strong and believe in a better future for yourself. Don't let yourself settle for temporary satisfaction that will set you back and make progress harder.

When your loneliness is stinging you, ask yourself, *Am I someone who would jump into a relationship or marriage for the wrong reason, or am I willing to wait for what's right?* I've met people in relationships who told me, "I wish I were single like you" or "Don't get remarried!" All relationships have challenges, but two people who care for, respect, and love each other will do everything to work things out without getting others involved or betraying their trust and love. They will push through their bad times together.

Some relationships struggle because people don't talk about their expectations beforehand. How would you feel if your partner wanted to maintain a relationship with an ex-lover? The two might have children to parent, but that doesn't mean they need to be hanging out or spending time together; the ex might want more than friendship.

What if the person you're interested in decides that he or she should be allowed to hang out with members of the opposite sex? That could be a temptation. No matter how strong a person is, some temptations might be too hard to resist. This is why it's important that two people interested in pursuing a relationship should have heart-to-heart conversations on the following scenarios.

- What do you consider emotional faithfulness? Are you fine with your mate sharing their personal business with someone they might be attracted to or vice versa? Emotional intimacy and physical attraction are ways people connect. Some people can be emotionally unfaithful to their mates simply by getting emotionally intimate with someone else, and that can be even worse than having an affair.
- Some people know their mates are cheating on them, being irresponsible with money, or manipulating them, but they stay in the relationship because they are afraid to be alone, and they feel trapped.
- Some jump into relationships despite the red flags and end up emotionally or physically abused.
- Some who have jumped into relationships end up losing the trust of their children because they sacrificed their children to keep their mates. When my kids were small, someone told me, "Men and women will come into your life, but if you treat your children right, they will always love and take care of you." I kept my kids close and sacrificed relationships.

- Some people sacrificed their children so they could be with a mate. As a result, many children and adults are emotionally scarred due to having been abandoned by their parents. Worse are those who physically harm their children for a mate. This is horrifying.
- There are people who had dreams and aspirations. The wrong connection stifled them because they hooked up with and ended up settling for mates with no such dreams, and they lose their aspirations.
- Some who were financially stable hooked up with financially irresponsible people and ended up ruining their fiscal security. Many will meet with financial struggles and have to rebuild, but sometimes, their mates will not care to help them in that matter. Be aware that many people have hidden agendas.

Don't become hopeless after reading these scenarios because happy and healthy relationships can successfully deal with and overcome such problems. These scenarios are to help point out why it's better to wait than jump into something before you really know yourself, what you want and the importance of establishing your boundaries.

I know waiting is very challenging but be patient and wait for that special one you can develop a relationship with if that's your desire. Don't jump into a situation and not know what you're getting into. Someone who loves you will protect your heart, sanity and will value and respect you. In the meantime, enjoy your time being single and don't allow others' negative comments or opinions to influence you.

Prayer

Father, come and be with me as I grow. Free me from the negative things I've heard. Guide and help me to just be me. Help me to be happy and at peace and feel your love for me in my state of singleness. I claim victory as I await the one you have for me who will love, protect, be loyal to, and treat me with the utmost respect. In Jesus's name I pray, amen.

⸮?⸮

CHAPTER 10

Things to Do to Avoid Pitfalls

Pitfalls? We've all experienced them, and I'm referring to emotional pitfalls that knock us off track. Pitfalls are anything that will cause you to stumble, not walk right, take away your peace, and cause some sort of emotional turmoil during your season of being single. Let's talk about how to avoid them.

Some music, TV shows, certain environments and people can be emotional pitfalls. You hear a song that makes you feel lonely or romantic or reminds you of someone, and you end up contacting that person, someone you shouldn't have. Music is very powerful and can influence you in many ways. Be careful what you listen to or watch and monitor your actions afterward. Avoid sexual music, movies, or any vices that will cause you to think of your singleness, your desire to have a mate, or anything that could cause you to devalue yourself.

Cut off those people who aren't good for you even if that's hard. Relationships with these people aren't going anywhere. It doesn't take long for someone to figure out if he or she wants to be in a relationship with you. If a woman doesn't want to commit to you, my dear fellow, you might want to find out why. Guys, a woman who doesn't want to commit to you is usually emotionally connected to another guy or has expectations you'll never meet.

Ask those who have been in relationships for a long time why they're not married; I've heard many such people say, "If it's not broke, why fix it?" I tell them, "If it's that good and you have no intentions of ending it, why not make it official and marry?"

If you're in a long-term relationship like that, ask yourself, *Where's this going? Are we in this forever or just until one of us gets tired and finds someone else?* If you can't answer these questions and you know your relationship isn't going anywhere, run and don't look back. Yes, some people have committed after seven years, and they had a plan for their future. Ask happy couples how long it took them to commit to each other? Every relationship and scenario are different.

More Pitfalls to Avoid

- Stay away from booty calls; they always end up hurting someone.
- Determine the people you need to stay away from because of their toxicity.
- Don't allow your emotions or needs to put you in a negative cycle.

I don't have time for toxic relationships or damaging cycles. I seek something real, meaningful, and mature. You cannot move forward with anyone who is unwilling to commit to you for whatever reason. People's actions and words will tell you where you stand with them and how they feel about you. Be aware and accept their reality for what it is.

Pitfalls are Real

Men and women who are seeking companionship can end up in pitfalls and chasing eye candy (Eye candy is anything that is appealing to one's visual desire. Beauty is in the eye of the beholder and each person's eye candy is different). People whom you are attracted to seem to say all the right things. Unfortunately, some of those people may be smooth and charismatic players, self-centered individuals some of whom are abusers. They will pull you in and then toy with your emotions, saying, "I didn't lead you on" or "I never told you we were in a committed relationship," when in reality their actions showed you something completely different. Take your time to find out if someone is a player who knows how to deceive you with his or her sweet talk and charisma but then withdraws from you for the next conquest; you could save yourself a lot of grief.

If you realize too late that you've fallen for someone like that, don't beat yourself up; figure out what you can learn from that experience to avoid similar experiences in the future.

You can protect your heart by first knowing what you want from a relationship, what you can give to one and then determining that you are ready for a relationship; that's when you can start looking for a mate whose actions and words line up. Here are some questions to ask and identify the red flags.

- Is someone only consistently communicating with you and responding to your inquiries?
- Is someone trying to hold onto ex-lovers as well as you?
- Is someone trying to make you feel bad because you aren't out there as he or she is?
- Is someone always justifying his or her actions with the opposite sex?
- Is someone always telling you that he or she isn't a player but constantly entertaining those attracted to them?
- Is he or she pulling you in but then pushing you away?
- Is he or she available to you only at certain times of the day or night?
- Is there nothing more to your relationship with this person than sex?
- Does anyone in that person's circle know about you? Have you met anyone close to them?

Think about your nonnegotiables and the answers you would like. As you evaluate the answers of others, be sure to evaluate yourself to make sure you aren't demonstrating any red flags. If you recognize some of these behaviors in yourself or someone you are involved with, don't beat yourself or that person up; just admit it about yourself or that person. You can change your ways or get out of a relationship with someone that has shown you many red flags. If they are not willing to address your concerns or do what it takes to make the relationship better, then you have to make the decision that is right for you. Some people may choose to stay while some may choose to move on.

People who are unwilling to commit are often manipulators who will do anything to satisfy their selfish needs including sex or companionship on their terms, not yours. They don't mind wasting your time or hurting your feelings. Stay out of their webs of deceit; that's much easier than getting out of them. Here are other types to be aware of and avoid.

- **Abusers:** People who mentally, physically, emotionally, and financially abuse others. Nothing's ever their fault. They'll try to blame you for the abuse you're feeling but won't accept any blame for their abusive behavior.

- **Controllers:** These are people who want to control what you do, how you dress, where you go, when you see your family—basically everything about you. Some controllers tell those they're trying to control that that's a sign of their love for them. This is different from your mate wanting to know where you are or what you're doing because he or she is concerned for your safety. I'm talking about someone who dictates where you go or what you can or cannot do.

- **Pessimists:** These are people who don't want to do anything with their lives and don't want you to try to help them do anything to improve their lives. They hate on others and make negative comments about them: "So and so thinks he's better than me" or "She got a lucky break she didn't deserve." They constantly make negative comments about things you or others want to do because they're dream killers.

How to Avoid Pitfalls

The way to avoid pitfalls is by identifying them. Who or what can get you off track? Who or what can cause you to lose sight of your goals? Identifying these people or things can help you spot pitfalls and avoid them. Here are some ways you can do that.

- **Pray or Meditate:** Not everyone subscribes to a religious faith, but prayer has certainly helped me find peace. You can pray for different things.

  o Strength when you are lonely

    Be strong and courageous, do not be afraid or tremble in dread before them, for it is the Lord your God who goes with you. He will not fail you or abandon you. (Deuteronomy 31:6 AMP)
    What then shall we say to all these things? If God is for us, who can be [successful] against us? He who did not spare [even] His own Son, but gave Him up for us all, how will He not also, along with Him, graciously give us all things? Who will bring any charge against God's elect (His chosen ones)? It is God who justifies us [declaring us blameless and putting us in a right relationship with Himself]. Who is the one who condemns us? Christ Jesus is the One who died [to pay our penalty], and more *than that*, who was raised [from the dead], and who is at the right hand of God interceding [with the Father] for us. Who shall ever separate us from the love of Christ? Will tribulation, or distress, or persecution, or famine, or nakedness, or danger, or sword? Just as it is written *and* forever remains written, "For Your sake we are put to death all day long; We are regarded as sheep for the slaughter."
    Yet in all these things we are more than conquerors *and* gain an overwhelming victory through Him who loved us [so much that He died for us]. For I am convinced [and continue to be

convinced—beyond any doubt] that neither death, nor life, nor angels, nor principalities, nor things present *and* threatening, nor things to come, nor powers. (Romans 8:31–38 AMP)

Turn to me [Lord] and be gracious to me, For I am alone and afflicted. (Psalm 25:16 AMP)

Do not fear [anything], for I am with you; Do not be afraid, for I am your God. I will strengthen you, be assured I will help you; I will certainly take hold of you with My righteous right hand [a hand of justice, of power, of victory, of salvation]. (Isaiah 41:10 AMP)

He heals the brokenhearted And binds up their wounds [healing their pain and comforting their sorrow]. (Psalm 147:3 AMP)

○ Sexuality

Do you not know that your body is a temple of the Holy Spirit who is within you, whom you have [received as a gift] from God, and that you are not your own [property]? You were bought with a price [you were actually purchased with the precious blood of Jesus and made His own]. So then, honor and glorify God with your body. (1 Corinthians 6:19–20 AMP)

Do you not know and understand that you [the church] are the temple of God, and that the Spirit of God dwells [permanently] in you [collectively and individually]? If anyone destroys the temple of God [corrupting it with false doctrine], God will destroy the destroyer; for the temple of God is holy (sacred), and that is what you are. (1 Corinthians 3:16–17 AMP)

Therefore I urge you, brothers and sisters, by the mercies of God, to present your bodies [dedicating all of yourselves, set apart] as a living sacrifice, holy and well-pleasing to God, which is your rational (logical, intelligent) act of worship. And do not be conformed to this world [any longer with its superficial values and customs], but be transformed and progressively changed [as you mature spiritually] by the renewing of your mind [focusing on godly values and ethical attitudes], so that you may prove [for yourselves] what the will of God is, that which is good and acceptable and perfect [in His plan and purpose for you]. (Romans 12:1–2 AMP)

You should pray about or meditate on the type of mate you want in your life—one who will honor, respect, and love you; be loyal to you; and support you in all you do. You have to make your own decision about the relationship you're looking for. It's not necessary to share all your business with others. It's good to get advice, but your decision about someone must be only yours.

Pitfalls are real and no matter how disciplined or strong you believe you may be, pitfalls are pits that you fall into unexpectedly. You might fall into a pitfall you weren't prepared for, but again, don't beat yourself up; just learn from the experience. Know your strengths and weaknesses so you'll be ready intellectually, logically, and spiritually to deal with your pitfalls. Be wise in all you do.

Prayer

God, help me avoid any pitfalls. Give me discernment and wisdom to handle different situations and people. Help me know who is for me and who is not. Guide my steps and be with me in all I do. I pray for my future mate as that person prays for me according to your Word. I bless you, God, and thank you for what you will do in my life, amen.

CHAPTER 11

Waiting and Preparing

By now, you've identified your issues, accepted that you need to focus on yourself, and made the commitment to prepare yourself to be emotionally and mentally ready for the mate meant for you if it's God's will. Some people are meant to be alone and they do not have a problem with being single. There is nothing wrong with anyone who makes the choice to remain alone.

No matter how long you have been single, if it is meant for you to be with someone, your time will come. I know people who were single for years after divorcing or being widowed but ended up marrying again. They had something in common—they knew what they wanted and wouldn't settle for less.

The state of singleness is not easy; I can say that from experience, but I look to the day when I will walk down the aisle and see true love in my handsome husband-to-be. I'll know he will honor and respect me for who I am. I will have spent enough time with him to know that he is an honorable, loyal, respectful, faithful, and godly man who will protect my heart while helping me grow. He'll love everything about me. This vision has helped me stay grounded, focused, and at peace. I want this vision—I won't settle for less.

While I wait for him, I'll focus on my spiritual, emotional, physical well-being, my professional growth and financial stability.

Here are things you can do to stay busy during your season of waiting, healing, and growing.

- dancing—salsa, line dancing, etc.
- practicing martial arts
- exercising at a gym or just walking
- taking Zumba classes
- joining a fishing club
- engaging in recreational activities (only legal and ethical)

  - painting
  - cake decorating
  - wine tasting
  - knitting
  - learning how to fix a car
  - learning a new language
  - shooting at a range
  - making pottery

- joining a club or meet up group

  - soccer
  - football
  - flag football
  - basketball
  - hiking
  - swimming
  - skating
  - karaoke
  - line dancing

- educating yourself about financial matters—IRAs, investing, life insurance, and so on
- reducing your expenses
- buying a car or house
- developing your spirituality

  - determining what faith you want to follow
  - reading the Bible

- ○ learning about other religions
- ○ speaking positives into your life such as "I am beautiful," "I am a success in all I do," "I am respectful and loving," and more.
- ○ posting your positive affirmations to remind yourself of who you are

- being saved by accepting Jesus Christ (Romans 10:9–11)
- reading the Bible and joining a Bible study group
- volunteering—at a hospital, orphanage, or home for the elderly for instance
- getting to know people by going to meet-up groups
- sharing the gospel on mission trips
- becoming fit and healthy—Are you at your ideal weight?
- go on walks if you do not like the gym
- getting a yearly checkup—a full body/blood check—and being checked for STIs (a must if you've had more than one sexual partner in a year)
- taking multivitamins
- maintaining a healthy diet that includes fruits and vegetables
- drinking more water and fewer sodas
- becoming and staying mentally and emotionally fit

- ○ Seek professional counseling if you feel unable to get rid of some negatives you have experienced.
- ○ Participate in different types of therapy that will help you find your peace such as acupuncture, past-life regression, spiritual retreats, or getting in tune with your inner spirit through prayer and fasting.
- ○ Stop being angry about the nonsense people have done to do to you because they were probably projecting their issues on to you.
- ○ Deal with childhood hurts or issues through therapy or meditation and prayer.

During your single season, focus on getting yourself ready for that wonderful mate who's getting ready for you. You're doing great! You can and will make it. You've taken the first step if you know what you need to do to get to know and heal yourself.

As you prepare yourself and wait, you will find greater inner freedom. You will be able to let go of the things that kept you bound. You will recognize that you are not identified by what people say but who you show others you are. This is a time of renewing your identity and learning to love yourself more than ever.

Prayer

Holy Spirit, guide me and show me how to overcome. Give me strength as I evolve.

CHAPTER 12

Keys to Finding Peace and Happiness in Singleness

You've been keeping yourself busy, you're ready to heal, and you've decided not to be sexually involved with anyone until marriage. Let's now turn to self-healing and growth.

Throughout this book, we've discussed different facets of healing, so let's bring them together step by step. I cannot say it will work for everyone because everyone's different and many variables come into play, but I and others have acquired peace through this method. These people are single and not sleeping around; they have found themselves, know what they want, and have complete peace. They are waiting on mates who are right for them.

Here we go with the process.

- You recognize that your life is not what you want it to be and have become frustrated. Take the time to pinpoint what is frustrating you. A person? Your job or career? Your finances? Your health or weight?
- Next, think logically and prayerfully about what you need to do to eliminate your frustrations. If it's your job and finances, plan to get a better-paying job, but remember that more money will not solve all your financial and work problems. Determine how much you need for your bills and expenses, and budget for them in a disciplined way.

- Take a hard look at whatever emotional baggage you're carrying. That's hard to do, so be patient with yourself.

    o Write down the emotional baggage you're carrying due to other relationships. Don't be in denial and tell yourself, *I'm fine. I'm over that.* If you're still thinking about a certain someone, stalking his or her page, thinking about what you could have done differently in that relationship, or praying that whatever relationship he or she is in now will end and you'll get him or her back, deal with your feelings!

    o Don't wish any harm on your exes; pray that God blesses them and help them find their way. Don't bring bad energy into your life by projecting it on others. If you wished harm on someone, renounce it and ask God for forgiveness. Let them go and focus on yourself. Your life will be a lot more peaceful and prosperous.

    o If you have a hard time dealing with your past hurts, consider seeking professional Christian counseling; that can be well worth it if you find the right counselor for you. You are not crazy for seeking counseling; what's crazy is never dealing with your issues. Counselors are doctors for the mind and heart just like a family practitioner does a physical to maintain the body and a dentist checks your teeth to maintain them.

- Determine what you can bring to a relationship, why you are a great catch and spouse material. Be real about whatever you need to change or improve on—get yourself together. Ask yourself if you'd want to marry someone like you. Being honest about that will allow you to move forward.

- Be realistic about what you want in a mate; no one, including you, is perfect, but you can decide to look for someone who complements you. Material goods are never on my list; inner qualities are. If a potential mate works hard and has faith in God, he or she will be able to provide. I'd take a man with fewer degrees but who is dynamic, hard-working, loyal, and respectful over a well-educated, wealthy man who has unappealing mannerisms.

- If you are constantly associating with people who are negative, don't do much, gossip, and have no ambition, you might be heading down that same path. Someone said, "Show me who your friends are today, and I will tell you who you will be tomorrow." You should never forget where you came from, but you should constantly evaluate yourself and your life.

The world is not designed for singles; society will be quick to remind you what you need to do to get into a relationship and the social norms of relationships, but you are a happily single individual who does not need to follow society's dictates. If you like hanging out with friends but then going home alone and binge-watch a couple of shows, don't think there's anything wrong with that. If you like to go on adventures by yourself or with a friend or two and have no interest in getting involved with anyone, you're fine. Enjoy your daring voyages. Enjoy your life and explore the world. If you are being responsible— not having sex with people or misleading others, there's nothing wrong with staying single despite what society says. Until you can be loved and respected for who you are, relish your singleness and never settle; you can never get the time or energy back that you give to someone in a relationship.

Every single person's experience of singleness will be different. It took a lot of healing and self-realization before I could find peace with being single; you have to find and maintain your sense of peace. It is important for you to understand that peace comes from within, letting go of all hurts, and not wishing harm on others. The energy you put out will return to you.

Prayer

God above, I need peace and guidance on how to let go of all my evil and ill thoughts of those who have hurt me. Help me forgive them and move on. I rebuke and renounce any ill thoughts I may have had about anyone, and I wish them well. Be with me as I begin this new journey of victory and peace. I claim the victory over my life and know that you are with me, amen.

⁇

CHAPTER 13

Building a Strong Foundation

Now that you know the importance of knowing yourself, it's time to build a strong foundation for yourself so you can find happiness and peace. Then, no one and nothing will be able to make you feel less than what you are. It is important to remember that you will never be perfect so don't stress yourself out thinking that you must be without any flaws. Similarly, others are not perfect and will make mistakes.

Some of what I have written is redundant, but I think the more you hear the information, the more likely it will stick in your mind. When it sticks, you'll be able to walk it out in your life.

Here are some ways to build a strong foundation.

- Find yourself and heal yourself; ask yourself,

    ○ What makes me happy?
    ○ Am I fine being alone?
    ○ What do I enjoy doing?
    ○ If money were not an issue, what would I do?
    ○ Am I working just to make a living?
    ○ Do I enjoy what I do?
    ○ If I were to die today, what would people say about me?
    ○ Am I living a life I'm proud of?
    ○ Where do I see myself in five or ten years?

o   Am I on track to accomplishing my goals?

o   Am I living with no regrets?

How did you do? Were you able to answer all the questions and smile, or did some of your answers frustrate you? Only you have the power to change how you feel. What can you change so you can comfortably answer these questions?

- Do some form of meditation; find which one makes you happy and gives your soul peace. For me, meditating can be lying in my bed and listening to scriptures, sitting on the floor and internally talking to God, sitting in my recliner and reading different meditation books, Praying and asking God for guidance, or taking a walk and admiring the beauty of all creation.

   I could not have made it this far without my relationship with Jesus Christ. At times, I wanted to curse someone out or get angry and retaliate, but I prayed, regrouped my thoughts, and carried myself accordingly. Meditating and having a relationship with Christ has been extremely crucial to my growth.

   Find a form of meditation and determine where your faith comes from. Mine comes from Jesus Christ, who gives me peace and signs when I need them.

- Part of getting to know yourself is getting yourself together in all ways—spiritually, mentally, financially, professionally, and physically. Let's take a look at each one and take a pulse check.

   o   Where are you spiritually? Are you as grounded in your faith or spiritual walk as you want to be? If not, what are you doing to turn that around? The fact that you aren't perfect shouldn't discourage you; realize that you'll always be a work in process. We are constantly evolving in a good or bad way till we die.

   o   Take a mental inventory. How are you feeling emotionally? The mind is the center of feelings of sanity and peace.

If you are full of hurt, hate, anger, and bitterness and have the desire to act out, you're not mentally fine. Figure out who has caused you to be angry or bitter; what are you doing to find a way to forgive them? Over the years, there has been an increase in mental illnesses and vicious acts of violence. I often wonder, if the people who were involved in the shootings and other acts of violence would have followed through, if they had taken a mental and emotional inventory. Some may say that such people have mental issues, but everyone is capable of evil acts in certain circumstances. If this were not true, the TV show *Snapped* would not have been created and court rulings of *Temporary Insanity* would not exist.

But anyone can turn this around; your mind is capable of more than you can imagine. Check your mind by checking your heart and your actions. If you're always angry, sad, hateful, bitter, or mean, ask yourself why and seek out help to cope with those emotions. I highly recommend you see a Christian counselor, a member of your clergy or finding a support group. The longer you wait to seek help, the more likely you will become capable of doing something you did not think possible. Maybe you're making everyone around you miserable right now! Get the help you need to become a better you.

○ Take inventory of your finances. Until your savings will cover your expenses for at least two years, you're not financially prepared to handle financial emergencies. Life comes with unpredictable scenarios, so make sure you can handle the unpredictable.

○ Take inventory of your work life. Are you happy with it? Too many say, "I hate my job!" or "I dread going to work!" If that's you, it's time to move on to another company or start your own. Constantly hating your job or the people you work with is a mind-set that is detrimental to your emotional and even physical health. I commend the millennials for taking a stance about their lives and careers; many do not stay anywhere for too long, and they'll readily quit their jobs when they become unhappy with them. Your health and sanity come first.

It can be very scary to contemplate switching jobs, but you can overcome your fears of taking that risk; the alternative is remaining at a job that will probably continue to stress you out. You have choices and should never be afraid to seek a promotion where you are or take a lesser-paying position elsewhere, if necessary. Consider starting a business, cutting down on your expenses, taking loans out so you can go back to school to get a new degree, or pursuing additional training that will help you land a more rewarding position.

One way or another, stop limiting yourself and making yourself and everybody else miserable. Change your mind and you will be amazed at how you can change your life.

- o Take inventory of your physical appearance. Are you happy with how you look? If not, what don't you like, and how can you change that? Don't compare yourself with others. If it is your weight, get out and start exercising. If it is your hair, color or cut it. You are in control and should be please with your appearance.
- o Keep in mind that this inventory process is about determining how you can create the best you that you can. You have to be happy with yourself and have inner peace.

- After you've given yourself a good look and worked on different areas of your spirit, mind, professionalism, finances, and physical appearance, find things you like to do and others who like the same things. Connecting with like minded people can be fun and help you learn about yourself.

  - o Join activities or social clubs—salsa, chess, soccer, or debating.
  - o Go to the movies or dinner by yourself.
  - o Join a poetry club or go to concerts by yourself.

- Find accountability partners, judgment-free friends who won't share your business with anyone. I have an accountability partner for my spiritual walk and another for self-growth. My friends know of each other but are not acquainted. I'm grateful for the way they hold me accountable to accomplish my goals. They don't ridicule me for my failures; rather, they encourage me to get back on track. Do you have someone who can do that for you?

- Travel. Yes, travel, and it doesn't need to be abroad. One way or another, leave the comfort of your home and community and go somewhere new. I've met so many people who have not explored even their immediate environments. Go visit someplace, anyplace new, and see it with your own eyes. When presented with the opportunity, visit other states and countries. Meeting others from different areas with different customs and habits can broaden your point of view.

- Pick up a new hobby or volunteer somewhere. The elderly in nursing homes or the kids in an orphanage would love your company. I volunteer at a hospital to play with children and cuddle infants; making them smile and praying God's mercy over them gives me joy. What would bring you joy? Is there something you have always wanted to do?

- Consider writing—poetry, a novel, a recipe book—whatever you desire to write. Take control of your life and happiness. When you don't have a plan or an idea of what you want to do, others will try to decide that for you.

- As you grow and learn about yourself, identify other areas in your life that you want to change for the better. Don't be afraid to get input from a close friend to tell you what he or she thinks are your best and not-so-good qualities. Don't take whatever that person says as gospel but just as a double-check to see if you've overlooked something about yourself that stands out to him or her. Make a list of your positive and negative qualities.

- Enjoy life; don't take yourself too seriously. Find people who will encourage you and lift you up when you're down. Never forget where you came from and treat others with respect. Give

God praise for how far you have come and everything he is going to do in your life. You're a success in the making!

Now that you've identified what you want to improve about yourself, think about what you would like in a mate in terms of his or her character, not in terms of his or her looks or bank account. Create a list of character traits you would like in a mate. Don't put down anything you can't offer. Different people desire different character traits. I could tell you that you want someone who is kind and respectful, loves his or her family, loves children, is selfless, and is a good listener—someone who would enhance your life. However, these traits are not desired by everyone. You must create your own list.

Think realistically about your negotiables and nonnegotiables such as religion, having children, and so on. Some want mates of a specific race or with no children. I once had a guy who told me he was interested in me but didn't want to be a father to my children; that relationship ended soon after, but I respected him for telling me up-front. I wasn't interested in anyone who was in the divorce process or dating multiple people; those were among my nonnegotiables.

Now that you have been provided with resources, tools, and information on how to take inventory of yourself and your life, it's time to begin loving yourself and walking into a better future for yourself. Take control of your emotions and singleness and give your life to God. It won't be easy, but it's well worth it. Don't compromise no matter how hard that may be; the consequences of settling are long lasting and unpredictable. Be love, be the person God created you to be. Know that you are not alone, and you can do this. If I can, so can you!

Prayer

God, thank you for delivering me of my past. Thank you for helping me create a better and brighter future. I receive all the blessings you have for me and am ready to be a blessing for others. In Jesus Christ's name I claim my victory!

?

CHAPTER 14

Wait! I Have Children!

At this point, you know the importance of knowing yourself and finding your peace. You have begun identifying what you like and don't like. You've created a list of the character traits you want in a mate. You've come a long way and are starting to feel good. You see a bright future ahead because you've taken the necessary steps to help you grow and improve yourself.

But wait! You have children! Can you still follow the same process described? Of course! The difference is that children will add a couple of more steps to the process of starting and developing a relationship with anyone.

Being a single mother of children was not always easy for me; any single parent can relate to that. After I received several negative comments on my state of being a single parent, it became very clear that some people did not look kindly on single parents. Some said, "You should have stayed married!" or "It's your fault that you're struggling!"

Single parents often hear such negative comments. At times, you may hear someone say, "I don't know how you do it." As the numbers of single parent households grow, it is important for society to understand that each household has a different story. Many think that single parents are just trying to find mates to and don't give their children the care and attention they require, but many healthy, successful people were raised by single parents. Besides my son and daughter, Jasmin and Aaron, I can think of Barack Obama, Halley Berry, Christina Aguilera,

Alicia Keys, Mariah Carey, Jodie Foster, Justin Bieber, Ben Carson, and so many more amazing actors, athletes, politicians, and medical professionals. Being a single parent can be difficult, but it's not a curse.

At times, I felt I was marked negatively because I was a single parent, so I began to write a book: *My Scarlet Letter—S—Being Single and a Single Parent*. Hester Prynne, the main character in Nathaniel Hawthorne's 1850 novel *The Scarlet Letter*, was convicted of adultery and made to wear a red *A* to announce her wrongdoing. No one should ever have to walk around feeling like Hester Prynne—ashamed of who they are or the circumstances they are in. Yes, people make mistakes, but it's not necessary for others to remind them of their mistakes. Some people are very hard on themselves and feel even worse whenever someone says something like that. In many cases, parents are single because of different reasons and divorce. Many people divorce for a variety of reasons; unfortunately, many are made to feel as if it were their fault, that they had done something wrong. People shouldn't be mistreated because of their life events.

I remember hating my life as a single parent because of things people would say about me, my future, or my children's future. I made some bad decisions, but who doesn't especially when they're young? Now that I am wiser and older, I understand the saying *Youth is wasted on the young*.

There are many good, hard-working single parents who take time to go out and relax; that doesn't mean they're being irresponsible with their children or looking for someone to solve their problems. The number of irresponsible single parents is much smaller than that of single parents trying to give the best life they can to their children. Irresponsible single parents have been affected by the anger, hurt, and pain they carry and are struggling to handle things better. I hope this book will help some of them cope better with their circumstances and help others have more compassion and respect for them.

Children are a blessing, but they can be a challenge. Raising children as a single parent is more challenging than doing that with the help of a spouse. Most single parents end up in a survival mind-set and can't think about anything except paying bills, putting food on the table, and making sure their children have what they need. For them, failure is not an option; they have no time for foolishness.

Some people are critical enough to tell a single parent, "No one will want to raise another person's children" or "Who would want to marry someone with so much baggage?" I learned to accept the hate shown to me and other single parents as ignorance. I realized it would be better to focus on helping singles love themselves than to worry about others' ignorance. I know men and women who have married single parents, some with multiple children. God will bless abundantly those who take on the challenge of loving someone's else's child.

It takes a very special and wonderful person to marry someone, love everything about him or her, and take on the parental responsibility for his or her children. If you are one of those men and women and you are treating your children with the utmost respect and love, may God bless you abundantly. Children need to feel safe, cared for and an abundance of love from their care takers.

How to Prepare Yourself with Children

Single parents have to make time to be with and love their children. I wish I could go back and redo some things I did with my children. Unfortunately, I was in survival mode and didn't understand that their hearts were broken and they needed my attention, too. I was so worried they would not do well in life that I would work my full-time job and do three or four part-time jobs to make sure I could provide for them. As a result, I became angry and bitter about many things; I felt I was not supposed to struggle, be single, or face the challenges that were before me. I just wanted the best life for my two kids. Despite my flaws, I am grateful that I was able to make sure they received good educations, develop a relationship with God, and knew that I loved them.

If you're a single parent, be sure to take time to cuddle with your little ones and let them know that you love them and that no matter what happens, they can never be replaced. Be careful what you say to them because they will remember it even if you didn't mean it; they'll take everything you say as fact.

Here are some things single parents should do for their children.

- Pray with them regularly to give them a religious and spiritual foundation.
- Help them love themselves by complimenting them and telling them you believe in them.
- Schedule time to be with your little ones, but keep in mind that the quality of that time is more important than its quantity. Make each moment meaningful, and don't fuss about matters while you're with them.
- Give them unconditional love while being fair, consistent, and firm. Disciplining your children is an important part of loving them.
- Teach them to respect their elders, but let them know that their bodies are special and that no one should ever touch them inappropriately. Have an open line of communication. They should never feel afraid to talk to you for fear that you will reject, won't protect or believe them. Too many children have been mistreated or abused and their parents did not protect them.
- Teach your child to be honest, respectful and to understand the damage that lies can cause. Don't wait till something happens to have these talks. Important talks should take place when there is peace and nothing to fear or issues to handle.
- Talk to your children about your future and explain that one day, you might bring someone else into your life who will be a good fit for the family. However, don't bring everyone you date home or introduce him or her to your children; that's a huge no. When I was dating as a single parent, my children did not know until they were in middle school and one of my daughter's friends made a comment which caused her to come home and question me. My children asked me if I had been dating and I was honest with them. They couldn't believe I

had kept that a secret from them, and it took discussions to get them to understand that I was not just *a mom* but also a woman. I can laugh about the whole conversation now, but it was not funny at the time.

- If you want to have other children, be careful what you say. I'll just say that I made some comments that I should not have on the subject. There were times I thought I wanted a third child, but I realized later that I should have kept such thoughts to myself. However, I'm grateful that children are resilient and can be forgiving.

- Make sure you are building a strong positive bond with your children. Keep your parenting duties a priority, but also reserve time for yourself by perhaps making sure they have a set bedtime. As much as you might want to go out or travel, your children's needs come first, and you should show them that.

- Teach your kids how to help you keep your house clean; cleanness is important.

- Determine how to introduce someone you start dating to your children. Do not say he or she is an uncle or aunt. Keep it honest and true—introduce your date as a friend until you determine an official title.

- If you decide to marry someone, ask your children if they would be comfortable calling him or her mom or dad or by a first name; that will be a discussion where the child(ren)'s thoughts and feelings should be respected. It will be a big step for everyone.

- Do not talk to your children about people you are dating as if your children were your friends. It's not their business to know if you didn't or did have a good time. Keep your conversations with your children on a parent-child relationship level. Set boundaries.

- Talk to the person you are interested in about your children to gauge if he or she likes children and would accept yours. It is important to determine if his or her values are similar to yours. If you're sure about your values, you'll be better at gauging someone else's values and determining if you are a good match in that respect regarding your children.

- Don't introduce anyone you're dating to your children until you're certain you're heading for a committed relationship. The meeting between that person and your children should be your final deciding factor of if the relationship will work. Reciprocating the same respect and mannerisms are important if you're dating someone who has children; that person will expect you to treat his or her children the same way you treat yours. Remember that all the children potentially involved did not ask for this situation.

Children are a blessing, but the world can make single parents feel as if they've done something wrong. Being single with or without children is very challenging, and every single parent's scenario is different, so no one handles his or her circumstances the same. Don't feel you have to do what everyone else is doing. Do your best, continue to push forward, and do not give up. Stay positive and ignore the ignorant comments.

When you meet someone with whom you think you could have a future, take it slowly with that person and your children; everyone involved will have to make some adjustments, so be clear with your children about your love for them and with anyone who will come into your life.

Prayer

God, I am grateful for my children, my blessings, and the opportunity to provide for them. My life might not be what I want it to be, but I am thankful that you are making a way when things seem confusing or challenging. I know you are here with us and will continue to guide my steps. Help me to properly prepare my children, and please guide me on this journey. I give you honor and praise for what you are going to do, amen.

CHAPTER 15

Married People and Preparing to Marry

So, you want to get married? That's wonderful! You should. Marriage is an absolutely beautiful union when it's between two willing, loving, and complete individuals. Don't let anyone tell you otherwise or that you shouldn't get married.

If you and someone love each other, you should marry and work together to make it last. Marriage is a stage of continuously trying to keep the flame going and never giving up on the love that brought the two of you together. Yes, marriage is hard, and you have to go into it for the right reasons. Any other reason than love and wanting to be with that particular person may add additional challenges.

One day, I will remarry; it'll be because of love, and it'll be great. I don't expect everything will always be perfect, but I'm willing to put in the effort to make it last.

Unfortunately, many people marry for lust rather than love, and there's a difference between the two. According to the Bible,

Love is patient, love is kind and is not jealous; love does not brag and is not arrogant, does not act unbecomingly; it does not seek its own, is not provoked, does not take into account a wrong suffered, does not rejoice in unrighteousness, but rejoices with the truth; bears all things, believes all things, hopes all things, endures all things. Love never fails; but if there are gifts of prophecy, they will be done away; if there are tongues, they will cease; if there is knowledge, it will be done away. (1 Corinthians 13:4–8 NASB)

This is one of my favorite passages because it explains love in its purest form. I'll offer you here some information about true love that comes from chapter 15, "True Love—Do You Exist?" of my book *Bad Girl Gone Good—Learning to Trust*

Love is one word with many interpretations. However, in Greek, it's covered by several words—*agape, phileo,* and *eros.*

Agape is the love of God or Christ for humankind. It's unconditional love, self-giving love, the kind of love God has for us and the kind children have for their parents. Phileo is a friendship type of love, a brother/sisterly love, one that expresses support and warmth. Eros is erotic love, physical lust.

You need to love your spouse with agape love, unconditional love, especially when things go wrong. You have to have phileo love so you can communicate respectfully and work things out as a couple; without it, marriages can be tougher to manage. You should also have some sort of eros love; if not, you'll be giving temptation a greater opportunity to destroy your marriage.

As you can see, you need more than superficial love (eros) if you want to experience love wholly. I hope that I've helped you understand what love is and that you will be more careful about telling someone, "I love you."

Marriage

Marriage can be a very beautiful union, but when there is no respect, trust, or commitment and loyalty, the hurt caused can run very deep. Third parties can of course destroy marriages, but marriages can also end when one or both spouses don't try to keep their relationship going. No matter how good a marriage starts off, it will require faith, trust, loyalty, respect, and commitment on both sides to keep going.

Single people can find challenges when dealing with married folks. If you're an attractive woman or man, some married people might get nervous and act as if you were going to try to steal their mates. However, a married person afraid of someone taking his or her mate is the one with a problem, perhaps the mate isn't trustworthy. If a person's spouse has never done anything to cause their mate to be insecure, then a single person would not be intimidating.

No one will be able to turn the heads of a husband or wife who are truly committed to each other. If a married man is trying to get involved with me, I'm not the problem; his attitude toward his relationship is. I would never tempt a married man or anyone else in a relationship because I don't like to share, and I am strictly monogamous. I believe in the sanctity of marriage and fear the wrath of my God, no one else. I refuse to get caught in a mess and ruin my reputation for a fling.

Single people who want to get married have to first respect the sanctity of marriage. No matter the temptation, it is extremely important to respect the sanctity of marriage. Always remember, what you do will come back to you and your relationship at some point. Worst would be if there are any consequences that would impact your children or future children. Do not participate in anything you wouldn't want to happen in your marriage.

Some married people are miserable, and that's very sad. Marriage is meant to be a beautiful union of two people that all others should respect and support. Those who decide to marry must cut off all exes and other distractions to keep their marriage sacred. Marriage gives us a sense of family, loyalty, security, trust, and love. When a marriage is destroyed or dysfunctional, everything else falls to pieces. I don't think married people realize how many singles are watching the marriages around them trying to determine if they should marry. I tell singles to support their married friends and their relationships by staying out of their business and not participating in confrontations. If you must be involved, make sure you are encouraging the couple to talk, support each other, and pray together. Encourage them to love and respect each other, remind them to treasure the love they started out with, and then stay out of it.

Listen to and learn from those who have successful marriages; I have. Here is the advice some such couples have offered me about marriage. I've changed their names, but I have their consent to share their information. They've been married for at least a year and up to over forty-five years. The following questions were asked,

- how long have you been married?
- why did you agreed to participate in my informal survey?
- how did you meet?
- how did you know you were in love and wanted to marry?
- what were some things you agreed upon to stay married?
- what were your hardest marital challenges and what helped you get through them?
- do you practice any sort of spirituality in your relationship?
- what characteristics (communication, respect, etc.) helped your marriage work?
- what they did you do to keep temptation at bay?
- what advice would you give to those wanting to get married and young married couples?

Here are their responses.

Edward and Eloise— "I Love Those Feet"

Edward and Eloise have been married for over ten years. Their love story began on a Sunday morning in the third pew at their church. Edward saw Eloise's feet first and hoped her face was as pretty as her feet (true story). They agreed to participate in the survey because they believe in love and Christ and that Christ is love.

Edward knew he was in love with Eloise when she started consuming all his thoughts, but love snuck up on her; she wasn't looking for a man and thought Edward was crazy! However, Edward assumed from day one that they would end up together. Eloise admitted that she stuck around only to see what would happen. Since they knew they wanted each other, they took themselves off the market and verbally committed to each other.

Six months after they met, Edward dreamed that the Lord had him ask Eloise for her hand in marriage, so he proposed, and she said yes. They decided that divorce was not an option, that they would always keep Christ first and keep family out of their marital business. They struggled with their desires for each other, but they wanted to stay in a right relationship, so getting married was the right way to handle that.

One of their hardest challenges was recognizing that both of them could not be in charge. One day, they discussed an issue and realized they had each other's best interests at heart and just needed to talk things out. They learned to submit to each other and hear each other out. They learned the importance of connecting with each other by touching and praying over their meals together and in church to bring their spirituality into agreement.

They told me that the following things made their marriage work: "We never lie to each other, we never cheated on each other physically or emotionally, and we selflessly please one another. We're not selfish in marriage, so it's us against the world."

They keep temptation out of their marriage by keeping their minds on Christ and on pleasing each other. The advice they would give any married couple, young or old, is that they should commit to Christ just as they commit to each other, honor that commitment by never giving up on their marriage and love each other as Christ loves the church.

Felisha and Baker— "Make Sure You Know the Other Person's History and How It Will Impact Your Future"

Felisha and Baker have been married for over fifteen years. They met on an internet dating site and felt that their growing relationship was God-ordained. They told me that one of the hardest challenges they faced was dealing with problems that came up in their marriage that challenged their faith in God.

Going to church together keeps their faith strong and communicating honestly about issues are ways they overcome. One of the blessings of their marriage is that they do not feel they struggle with temptation.

Their advice for young married couples is to swallow their pride, overlook the small stuff, be humble, and don't do anything they'd later want to lie about or hide. They'd tell them to understand that they can't change their spouses, only themselves.

The advice Felicia and Baker would give to a couple thinking about marriage is to be aware of each other's history, some of which could have implications for their marriage. They should make sure they complement each other emotionally, financially, and particularly spiritually. It is important to understand where you and your partner are and not believe you will be able to change each other.

Olivia and Western—"Giving It All for Love"

Olivia and Western, who met in a bar, have been married for over fourteen years. They separated for about nine months after which they got back together; they've been trying to work things out since.

They decided to participate in this survey because they wanted people to know that any marriage takes work. They wanted to share their story because they felt that reading about how others overcame their problems helped them.

They were always crazy attracted to each other and fell in love many times. They married when Olivia became pregnant. They went through different phases in their marriage, so the reasons they stayed together varied with that. They're in therapy because they struggle with communication.

The greatest challenge they faced was when Western decided he wanted a divorce but was going back and forth with Olivia about that and started cheating on her mentally. Olivia felt that that was worse than physical cheating. To make things worse, Western would lie to Olivia.

After she saw Western going to a hotel with a woman, she went into therapy with the support of family and friends and decided to cut off all communication with him and just move on. When Western realized he was losing Olivia, he told her that it had been a big mistake and asked her to come back. With therapy and love, they're trying to work through their difficulties.

They do not practice any religion or attend religious services together though one is a member of a denomination and the other is spiritual.

They were very transparent about how they were working through their marriage; they admit that they are "just winging it, and every day is a new day."

Olivia stated that to help their marriage, she has to "wake up and decide to put all my insecurities aside, make myself vulnerable, and hope we stay together." They agree that it's a challenge to move past the infidelity, but they're willing to try. It is a conscious decision that has to be made every day. They believe in the importance of communication.

Being faithful was not an issue for Olivia because she was always so busy with her children's activities that she couldn't even think about cheating.

Some of the advice they would give to a young married couple is this.

"Marriage is a journey. Who you are and what your relationship is today will change, evolve. You will have some bad years, not just some bad days. But if you love each other, you should wait out the bad times and have hope for good times. It is during the challenging times that many people give up because no one really wants to do the work to save their relationship. It is always easier to quit and start over. But how many times are you going to quit and start over? It takes two to make a marriage work particularly through bad times, so keep pushing through them rather than give up; that's the last resort."

Olivia and Western believe that society has convinced some married people that their spouses are replaceable, so they should wake up each day deciding to stay together.

Here's the advice they give to folks who want to get married: "It's unfortunate that it's so easy to get married and hard to get divorced. The process should be reversed. Relationships are harder than just getting married."

They don't believe it's necessary to spend a lot of money on a ring: "Don't go nuts on a ring. Five thousand bucks? Y'all nuts. It's a symbol." Same with spending so much on a wedding. Spend more time on each other than money on expensive rings and costly weddings.

Sam and Candie—"The Friend Connection"

Have you ever had a friend introduce you to someone and wonder if it could possibly work out with that someone? A mutual friend introduced Sam to Candie at a party; they dated for a while, but then they broke up. Nothing like a breakup to make you realize you miss and want to be with someone. During their time apart, they realized they loved each other and decided to get back together. They've been married for over ten years and have a couple of kids.

Sam and Candie believe that losing close loved ones is the hardest thing in a marriage. Healing from such a loss is an ongoing process and talking to each other helps. They feel it's important not to rush the grieving process but remember to practice empathy and be mindful of the process.

They attend church and pray as a family. They listen to music and connect with nature to help them maintain their peace. They believe it takes communication, honesty, patience, empathy, and more to make any marriage work.

In their ten years of making their marriage work and supporting each other, they learned it was important to acknowledge any signs of temptation so they could avoid it. They don't expect each other to be perfect; they work together on their conflicts rather than running to people outside their marriage to vent or to find solutions. They believe the answers will emerge when working together to make the marriage work. They're open and flexible with their ideologies and try to see each other's point of view even if they don't always agree. It is important not to be rigid and be able to see the other person's point of view.

The advice they'd give those who want to get married is to make sure they have the right intentions going into marriage and prepare for it by working on making peace with any concerns or issues from your past rather than dwelling on them. Being married is not easy, but you can make it work. It is important to keep people our of your business and communicate honestly while having patience with each other.

Quincy and Emilien—"Making It to Forever"

Can you imagine being married for over forty-four years? Quincy and Emilien can. They agreed to participate in this survey because they saw it as an opportunity to share their experiences about being married. They hope their story will benefit those contemplating marriage.

Emilien's family shared a picture of her with Quincy, and the rest is history. Quincy started calling and communicating with Emilien over the phone. After he went to Haiti to actually meet her, they married soon after.

Forty-four years later, Quincy and Emilien still have a good marriage because they keep God in the center of it and do their part to make it work. They have differences of course, but they said, "If you have respect, trust, understanding, communication, the ability to compromise, honesty, forgiveness, and love in your marriage, it will survive. We learned to pray to God before making any decision and ask Him to guide and direct us. He has not failed us."

Their faith and religion are the foundation of their relationship. They grew up Catholic, but in 2002, Emilien felt the need to leave the Catholic Church for another denomination, but Quincy remained a Catholic. That did not change their belief and trust in God. She said, "We put God first in everything we do, and we pray together. Sometimes, I attend his church, and sometimes, he attends mine." They've learned to make compromises and decide things together.

Here's the advice Quincy and Emilien would give to anyone planning on marrying.

1. Keep God in the center of your relationship and ask Him for wisdom.
2. Acknowledge that nobody is perfect.

3. Show respect to one another.
4. Pursue and show understanding.
5. Build trust and honesty in your relationship.
6. Develop the willingness to forgive.

Luke and Sarah—"The Second Time's a Charm"

Sarah was divorced, but she knew she wanted to be married again. However, this time, she wanted her marriage to be led by God. She was not in any hurry and was minding her own business when some friends decided to introduce her to Luke.

Sarah and Luke, who will soon be celebrating ten years of marriage, participated in this survey because they'd heard of so many marriages that failed and have heard that many people don't believe marriage is worth it anymore.

Sarah wants people to know that it is possible to find love and happiness after divorce. Sarah is a firm believer in the beauty, happiness, and personal growth that can occur in a healthy marriage, and she felt it was important to be a part of something that gave credibility and hope to those who wanted the same.

Sarah and Luke knew they were in love and wanted to marry because they had friendship, a sense of peace in their relationship, shared similar values, and had lots of laughter. Most important, they wanted each to do his or her best while becoming the best for each other; which led them to realize they were better together.

Sarah knew she was in love when she saw how kind Luke was about expressing his concern for her well-being. His generosity too made it easy for her to fall in love with him. Once they got married, they decided that the way they'd stay married would be to take some time off when things or decisions became difficult to manage and later revisit the issues together. They don't force things that don't seem right despite their emotions about it—big and small decisions alike.

They believe each other and honor what the other thinks and feels even when it doesn't align with what either believes at the moment. She and he will talk about things, but she will give way to his purpose and God-given responsibility to lead her in their marriage.

Sarah shared that one of her hardest challenges was learning to trust again. She had a hard time letting go of her memories of her previous marriage, but she did so by choosing to believe in Luke and remembering that his actions always lined up with his words. She learned that she did not have to be fearful or exert control because she had a willing and attentive partner. Getting through those times was a challenge for them, but Luke was patient and allowed Sarah to go through the process of releasing her fears.

Faith is a big part of Sarah's and Luke's relationship. They have been involved in various churches because they moved a lot, but they know that their lives and marriage must be grounded in Christ to survive. They pray and talk to and about God daily. Some of the characteristics they both practice in their marriage to make it work are these.

1. Keep each other first as spouses before anything and anyone.
2. Communicate and allow for differences and individuality.
3. Encourage each other's strengths.
4. Give each other the latitude to meet his or her individual needs.
5. Keep others out of your marriage.
6. Don't look for advice from others and especially from family and friends about your marriage.

Sarah and Luke feel it's important to set boundaries for anyone who could negatively impact their marriage, so they don't entertain situations or people that would cause each other to feel discomfort or doubt. They always consider each other.

Here's advice Sarah and Luke give to young married couples.

"Never put anyone before your spouse ever, and always be transparent with one another. Invest in each other's dreams and visions for life. Demonstrate to each other that he or she is a participant in and contributor to your dreams.

"The advice we give to married couples is to seek counseling if you need it; that's a healthy attitude to have. Don't look at the world's view of marriage because it's not real. Expect trials but believe in your ability to get through them even when you're at your weakest. Learn to recognize your selfish traits that get in the way of your solving problems together, and call yourself out so your partner can deal with his or her own stuff. Do not blame each other for anything; just be humble because life is hard."

Prayer

God, I come before you and lift up each of the married couples who have shared their testimony to help me and others grow. Bless their unions and help others to be blessed by their stories. May the testimonies shared bless young couple, saves marriages and helps build stronger marital unions. Help me become ready and able to live according to the advice they have given. I give you honor and praise, amen.

？

CHAPTER 16

Love

Love! Love? Love is a deep feeling that cannot be erased, is deep, pure, everlasting and true. We were created in love for love by God when we were created in His image. We learn how deep and pure God's love is through the death and resurrection of Jesus Christ. Jesus was a man that was without sin and willingly died for all of our sins. Can anyone truly say they would be willing to give their life for all those who mistreated, lied, abused, betrayed, or wished harm upon them? That is a difficult request. Yet, God loved us so much, He had Jesus do it. Jesus did it because He loved the church and the church is a representation of us. Is it possible for a man and woman to love each other as Christ loved the church (us)? Even when we did not deserve His love and mercy, it was granted. Read His Word and feel the love:

And God said, Let us make man in our image, after our likeness: and let them have dominion over the fish of the sea, and over the birds of the heavens, and over the cattle, and over all the earth, and over every creeping thing that creepeth upon the earth. And God created man in his own image, in the image of God created he him; male and female created he them. (Genesis 1:26-27 ASV)

Every one that is called by my name, and whom I have created for my glory, whom I have formed, yea, whom I have made. (Isaiah 43:7 ASV)

Looking for the blessed hope and appearing of the glory [a]of the great God and our Saviour Jesus Christ; who gave himself for us, that he might redeem us from all iniquity, and purify unto himself a people for his own possession, zealous of good works. (Titus 2:13-14 ASV)

But God commendeth his own love toward us, in that, while we were yet sinners, Christ died for us. (Romans 5:8 ASV)

For we are his workmanship, created in Christ Jesus for good works, which God afore prepared that we should walk in them. (Ephesians 2:10 ASV)

For God so loved the world, that he gave his only begotten Son, that whosoever believeth on him should not perish, but have eternal life. For God sent not the Son into the world to judge the world; but that the world should be saved through him. (John 3:16-17 ASV)

Jesus was born just so He could die to save us from our sins because God loved us despite our imperfections. God loved us so much that He wanted us to have the opportunity to get back into a good relationship with Him. Can we truly say that we have loved anyone and willing to make a huge sacrifice? Have you ever experienced a love so deep and pure? Most parents would say they've experienced this love during the birth of their child(ren) and I would definitely agree. The love of a parent and child is undeniable. The minute the baby is placed into your arms, it is as if the world stops and all you want to do is love and protect it. Is it possible to feel this kind of love for a mate? I have met couples whom you can see the love in their eyes for each other and know that there is nothing but trust, respect, and admiration. To see and be in the presence of such love is beautiful, refreshing and comforting.

True love is not a love that can be erased, ignored, or fall out of. People who are secure in themselves will be able to recognize this love, grab it and do everything they can to keep it. While a person who is insecure and full of emotional baggage will try to run from this love because they do not understand it, know how to deal with it, or are simply afraid of it. However, no matter where a person is, you cannot run. The person may be able to make the love dormant, but it never leaves or disappears. Once the love takes a hold of the heart, it does not leave but haunts if not faced and will always be remembered as *the love that got away.*

It is sad that people are willing to let something so beautiful go because of fear and different baggage and choose to live with regret. As stated by the married couples, love is not easy and requires work to overcome the hard times. Even a love that starts beautifully, will have trials and tribulations. Adam and Eve, the two people who were perfect, still messed up. Yet, we, who were born into sin and imperfection, expect to be perfect. Imagine that?

If you find true love with someone who is loyal, respectful, dedicated, and willing to pray and be with you despite the hardships and fear, hold on tight. Love is a journey with ups and downs. Love is beautiful and free. True love does not control, manipulate, disrespects, or betrays. If anything, it is the complete opposite. True love is freedom to be you and knowing there is someone that respects, will protect, encourage, pray, support and evolve with you.

It takes two people who are willing to be committed to their love and the relationships. True love is breath taking and not just sexual. It is when two people are willing to do whatever it takes to be with each other and forsaking all others to protect their love and relationship. Love makes you imagine the best in the other person and when something goes wrong, you pray for clarity and direction of how to fix the situation. It is not easy, but it does take two people willing to put in the work. Love will blind you to the other person's flaws and cause you to pray for them, even when they do not deserve it. But, isn't that what Christ did for us? When the love is reciprocated, it makes you feel as if the impossible can be accomplished because that person believes and supports you.

Love must be reciprocated for it to feel complete, pure, and beautiful. It is the worst when the love is not reciprocated. You begin questioning *why and how could I love a person that cannot reciprocate the respect, love, and loyalty? How did I manage to fall so deep that I am unable to get myself out and move forward?* The battle within begins.

It is my prayer that everyone who reads this book will be blessed with a love that is reciprocated, pure, true, and filling. May the love have a bond and commitment that is sealed with loyalty, respect, trust, confirmation, dedication and may not be broken by any third party or situation. May the couple work together to help each other grow spiritually, academically, financially, physically, and relationally.

True love is beautiful in every way. There will be trials, but with prayer, respect, dedication to each other, loyalty, and a commitment to the relationship, any couple will be able to overcome. Anything of value and worth will always require hard work. True love is a deep feeling that cannot be erased because it is pure and everlasting. It takes the two people who genuinely believe in their love and commitment to make it last while withstanding all obstacles. Until you find that person that is willing to give it their all for you and you are willing to reciprocate, wait and be patient. God has never failed.

Prayer

Lord, help me to wait on that true and pure love. If there is anything in me that would hinder me from seeing that love and keeping me from being able to reciprocate, open my eyes. Help me to be ready. Prepare my mate and help them to be willing to be true in every way. I want the love that you created for me without any hinderances. In Jesus' name I pray.

?

CHAPTER 17

Let It Begin

My learning how to heal and become whole has been a journey. Now we're going to begin to learn to love ourselves because in the end, we are the church showing and teaching others what love is.

In everything you do, start with prayer and meditation so you can be at peace in all you do. You are not doing anything in your life for anyone but you. You are the key to your happiness, and you can shine your light in a dark world. If you love yourself, you can be an example to those who do not know or are seeking an example.

It took me a while to recognize that I didn't love myself as I should. I needed to learn how to set boundaries, be silent, and determine if what was truth for others was good or bad for me. I learned that I needed to eliminate anything that was inhibiting my peace. Your peace is priceless, and it should not be compromised especially if you're single.

Below are some strategies and scriptures to encourage you to learn to love yourself.

Prayer

Remove self and increase in me, Holy Spirit, amen.

The Lord wants us to stand up and love ourselves so we can be examples for others and be a church that exhibits love to all.

These scriptures tell us how we were created in God's image.

Then **God** said, "Let us make man in our **image**, in our likeness, and let them rule over the fish of the sea and the birds of the air, over the livestock, over all the earth, [Hebrew; Syriac all the wild animals] and over all the creatures that move along the ground." (Genesis 1:26; whole chapter here)

So **God** created man in his own **image**, in the **image** of **God** he created him; male and female he created them. (Genesis 1:27; whole chapter here)

You are special and a beautiful generation of people. You must recognize that the world does not love us because we have Christ in us. Jesus said,

"If the world **hates** you [disciples], keep in mind that it **hated me first**." (John 15:18; whole chapter here)

You were made to do great things. Don't be afraid to be different, because Jesus was different. If you are doing the will of God and not conforming to the world, you will face trials and tribulations. Even the people you love may turn against you if they aren't walking in the Word. Keep your head up, and know that God will give you rest.

But you **will** cross the Jordan and settle in the land the LORD your **God** is giving you as an inheritance, and he **will give** you **rest** from all your enemies around you so that you **will** live in safety. (<u>Deuteronomy 12:10; whole chapter here</u>)

When people think they are going to destroy or bring you down, God will bless you, even in a bad situation. He says it right here.

You intended to harm **me**, but **God** intended it for good to accomplish what **is** now being done, the saving of many lives. (<u>Genesis 50:20; whole chapter here</u>)

Be proud to be young, old, black, white, Haitian, or whatever you are because that is just flesh. When you are a new child in Christ, you are no longer flesh but are being guided by the Holy Spirit.

But you will receive **power** when the **Holy Spirit** comes on you; and you will be my witnesses in Jerusalem, and in all Judea and Samaria, and to the ends of the earth. (<u>Acts 1:8; whole chapter here</u>)

Christ wants you to prosper, not perish. God wants to bless you for being faithful and helping others to come to know who He is. Those who do not accept Jesus Christ as the Son of God who died for their sins will not get into the kingdom of heaven.

But what does it say? "The word is near you; it is in your mouth and in your heart," that is, the word of faith we are proclaiming: That if you confess with your mouth, "Jesus is Lord," and believe in your heart that God raised him from the dead, you will be saved. For it is with your heart that you believe and are justified, and it is with your mouth that you confess and are saved. (Romans 10:8–10)

First, make sure you are saved, and then reach out to those you love. If you want to see them in heaven, make sure they confess with their mouths.

When we love ourselves, we will take care of ourselves. We are not going to just defile our bodies. No ... We're going to take care of and respect ourselves. We are not going to let a man or woman treat us with disrespect or as if we were second rate. No ... We are children of the Most High, God the Father, and we will be treated like royalty. We will increase by keeping our spirits fed with the scriptures. We will be examples for others and not just preach the Word.

When we realize how blessed we are, we will want to bless others. As we grow, we will connect with others who want to grow and find a church that will help us grow. We should remember that there are no churches without issues.

We should give to the church because that's the place we are being fed the Word and being taught how to become disciples of Christ. The church must be blessed financially to do the works that God wants its leaders to do. It's not for us to judge what they are doing but to pray and trust that God is guiding them to do what is right and spend their finances accordingly.

How can you get yourself right to be blessed and to bless others? Let us all get our priorities straight and begin to be blessed. Here are values to live by.

1. God: Put Him first and foremost
2. Our families: We are better and stronger in numbers than as one, and they give us a reason to work hard.
3. Education: Get knowledge so you don't perish because of a lack of it; learn a trade and how to run a business so you can increase yourself and get out of the "I must work for the man" mentality.
4. Money: Don't spend every dollar you get; that's a poor man's mentality. Save some money, and stay out of debt.
5. Property: Acquire as much property as you can so you can leave an inheritance for your children and their children.

Now you know what you need to do to start a spiritual revolution. Give God the glory because you are free to be you—different, loving, and prosperous. When you walk with God, He will bless you.

Delight yourself in the LORD and he will give you the **desires** of your **heart**. (Psalm 37:4; whole chapter here)

THE COMMITMENT CHALLENGE

As you are moving into your new season of self-love, peace, and waiting for the mate who was meant for you, take this challenge and see what God will do. I guarantee it will be a challenge, but the wait will be worth it. So let's see what happens. The information about "True Love Waits" is not my writing, but I believe in and support this document: http://www.lifeway.com/tlw/.

Believing that true love waits, I make a commitment to God, myself, my family, my friends, my future mate, and my future children to a lifetime of purity including sexual abstinence from this day until the day I enter a biblical marriage relationship.

The Five Commitments of True Love

- To God: "Jesus replied, 'Love the Lord your God with all your heart and with all your soul and with all your mind'" (Matthew 22:37).
- To yourself: "And the second is like it: 'Love your neighbor as yourself'" (Matthew 22:39).
- To family: "Let your gentleness be evident to all. The Lord is near" (Philippians 4:5).
- To friends: "Greater love has no one than this, that he lay down his life for his friends" (John 15:13).
- To your future mate and children: "Flee the evil desires of youth, and pursue righteousness, faith, love and peace, along with those who call on the Lord out of a pure heart" (2 Timothy 2:22).

DAILY AFFIRMATION

- I am at peace with my state of singleness.
- I love myself.
- I am unique; there is no one else like me.
- I am able to accomplish anything I set my mind to.
- I am full of love, joy, and peace.
- I am a child of the Almighty.
- I am a wonderful person.
- I am forgiven and am able to forgive others.

Printed in the United States
By Bookmasters